E-BUSINESS PRIVACY AND TRUST

PLANNING AND MANAGEMENT STRATEGIES

Paul Shaw

John Wiley & Sons, Inc.

New York • Chichester • Weinheim • Brisbane • Singapore • Toronto

ISBN: 0-471-41444-1

Printed in the United States of America.

10 9 8 7 6 5 4 3 2 1

ABOUT THE AUTHOR

Paul Shaw is editor and publisher of *Computing & Communications: Law and Protection* and *Assets Protection*, which covers internal controls, audits, and investigations. He is the author of *Managing Legal and Security Risks in Computing and Communications.* He is also co-author of *Fraud Awareness Manual, Forensic Accounting Handbook, Executive Protection Manual, Corporate Crime Investigation,* and *Avoiding Cyber Fraud in Small Businesses.*

CONTENTS

Preface   ix

Chapter 1   Marketing Versus Privacy   1

Chapter 2   A Primer on Privacy Law   19

Chapter 3   Healthcare Law Mandates Security   39
             and Privacy

Chapter 4   Privacy of Personal Financial   47
             Information

Chapter 5   Internet Privacy for Children   57

Chapter 6   European Union Privacy Protection   65
             Mandate

Chapter 7   Information Privacy and Compliance   71
             Programs

Chapter 8   Internal Protection Controls   85

Chapter 9   Creating and Communicating Policies   101

Chapter 10   Digital Signatures Liberate   117
             Electronic Commerce

Chapter 11   Biometric Security Systems   123

Chapter 12   Encryption Security for Electronic   135
             Commerce

Chapter 13   Protecting Proprietary Information   143

CONTENTS

Chapter 14   Secrecy and Noncompete   159
              Agreements

Chapter 15   Computer Insurance: Risks and   167
              Protection

Chapter 16   Audit Checklists and Monitoring   175

Glossary   195

Selected References   209

Selected Websites   215

Index   219

PREFACE

E-business is basically using the Web as another channel for business transactions with customers. E-business means using the Web to cut transaction costs, increase efficiencies, create innovative products, speed products to market, improve services, and enhance customer relationships.

Unfortunately, the Web has not been a fully secure or private place to do business, and until recently, it was nearly lawless. E-business can thrive only when transactions and customer or consumer information is protected and assured of privacy.

E-Business Privacy and Trust provides concise, clear, and cogent discussions of privacy law and the array of security technologies and services designed to create trusted, private consumer and business transactions. In this book, you will discover how to:

- study and assess privacy risks across operations handling personal consumer information

- create an effective company privacy policy

- establish internal controls and physical safeguards for information privacy

- audit privacy controls and information security measures

- monitor company privacy operations and practices and those of affiliates and third-party contractors

- keep current on the growing number of local, state, federal, and international laws governing privacy

PREFACE

Below is an overview of specific chapters in this book.

* * *

As discussed in Chapter 1, there is a growing public awareness that personal privacy encompasses the right to shield personal information from commercial interests. Anti-gathering techniques, in the form of information privacy products, are reviewed.

Chapter 1 also analyzes specific privacy policies, seals, and standards for websites, including the new standard, Platform for Privacy Preferences (P3P), and methods for collecting and building dossiers of personal information on site visitors. How consumer website traffic information is captured is an important privacy issue (see Chapter 5). It is vital to establish ongoing monitoring of the relationship between stated website privacy policies and activities of marketing, sales, or affiliated agents that could be counter to the policy.

Chapters 2 through 5 discuss the tort and constitutional origins of a right to privacy, as well as recent information privacy legislation covering financial and healthcare institutions and children's activities on the Web.

In Chapter 5, I have also included discussions of potential liabilities in operating a website, providing legal "rules of the road" for electronic commerce.

Chapter 6 explores the European Union's Privacy Protection Mandate and its effects on both U.S. companies doing business in Europe and privacy policy in general.

Chapters 1 through 9 use the framework for protection and compliance provided by the Treadway Commission's Committee of Sponsoring Organizations (COSO) on internal controls and the due diligence requirements of the *Federal Sentencing Guidelines for Organizations* (FSGO). These have become the standards for developing compliance and assets protection programs. Both COSO and the FSGO call for liability exposure inventories, policies, communication/education, internal controls, safeguards/security, reporting mechanisms, investigations, monitoring, and auditing.

Chapters 10 through 12, on digital trust, cover physical, network, and transactional security measures. Chapter 10 covers the security and legal implications of the electronic signature law for e-commerce transactions. Chapter 11 discusses identification measures that run from simple passwords to biometrics, and Chapter 12 covers encryption to secure transmission. I examine the use, efficacy, and problems of these security systems.

Chapter 13 examines the benefits of using trade secret law to establish programs that ensure the security and privacy of consumer and business information. Chapter 14 describes secrecy/confidentiality agreements and their use in protecting proprietary information.

Chapter 15 discusses the emergence of insurance policies for Internet and website operations that cover intellectual property infringement, computer hacking, and breaches of security for credit cards. Specific and blanket insurance policies relevant to computer-related crime and protection are surveyed.

Chapter 16 provides a set of audit checklists covering company liability exposures, compliance programs, and the security of information systems.

Throughout this book are detailed checklists on due diligence; legal liability exposures; security vulnerability assessments; and audits of management controls, monitoring systems, and legal compliance.

Website and Internet-related operations must include both a records management and a disaster recovery program. Records management should cover the backup, storage, and retrieval of electronic records generated by the website. Disaster recovery normally applies to a planned response to a data center catastrophe, yet a website should have its own plan that can work within the larger organizational plan. Chapter 16 includes extensive checklists covering the basic components of an internal control system for Internet and website operations, as well as computer facility management.

1

MARKETING
VERSUS
PRIVACY

Trust has become the make-or-break element of e-business; those with the best reputation for maintaining the privacy and security of consumer and business information will prosper. Without adequate privacy and security measures, e-businesses face the risk of litigation, negative publicity, and loss of customer loyalty. *E-Business Privacy and Trust* is a guidebook to how a business can develop an information protection program and how such a program can protect and enhance a company's reputational capital. Privacy and compliance law and security technology are discussed in concise, plain English.

Privacy and security are vital to the creation of trust and confidence in electronic business. This is true whether the company website operates business-to-consumer or business-to-business. Website operators must protect the confidentiality of information gathered about site visitors. Businesses also need to protect Internet transaction data and proprietary information. The payoffs for having strong privacy are customer loyalty and a shield from potential legal liability. Failure to protect consumer privacy on the Internet could easily undermine consumer confidence and retard the growth of e-business.

In nearly all discussions of privacy issues—in polls, legislation, privacy policies, contracts, and website visits—key words and phrases keep popping up. *Permission marketing* is often at the center of privacy debates and remains a critical unresolved privacy issue, particularly in legislation on privacy and in consumer privacy policies.

PERMISSION MARKETING: OPT OUT VERSUS OPT IN

Website privacy policies are often posted with one of two options for the consumer: opt out and opt in. Permission marketing uses these options to obtain personal information for marketers. Under the opt-out option, the consumer may refuse the information collecting and use arrangement. Opt out puts the burden of protecting personal information on the consumer. Under opt in, the consumer affirmatively agrees (usually in writing) to the specific collection and use of personally identifying information. This is the strongest demonstration of informed consumer consent. Opt in is perhaps the key issue for target marketers and behavioral profilers, because it is more expensive than an opt out and may require more and costly communication with a consumer. Opt in may involve "doing a value exchange" of gifts, prizes, money, or a few merchant coupons or using registration, surveys, or contests to get more information from the consumer.

CONSUMER ATTITUDES ABOUT PRIVACY

A 1995 poll conducted by Louis Harris Associates found that 83 percent of American adults are concerned about privacy invasions; 53 percent are very concerned about such threats. (The poll involved 2,506 consumers over the age of 18 and had a potential error factor of plus or minus 2 percent.) Consumers expect the highest degree of privacy in financial relationships (72 percent) and health information (71 percent). Those who indicated that privacy protection measures were very important and somewhat important totaled 94 percent for health organizations and 93 percent for financial services companies. Consumers who are most concerned about privacy are those with incomes above $35,000, college graduates, and those with postgraduate education.

A March 1998 Harris poll on privacy found that 78 percent of people using the Internet said they would use it more if they felt there was adequate protection of personal information. In March 2000, a poll by the Boston Consulting Group found that nearly half of the 80 million Internet users are women, who rate convenience as the main reason for using the Internet. Although consumers make repeat visits and make purchases from a few preferred sites (usually fewer than 10), a bad experience with any site could quickly end the relationship. These consumers wanted to see third-party verification of the company-stated privacy policies and security measures.

Odyssey, a market research firm, reported the results of a survey of online households in May 2000. Respondents to the survey on the best way to ensure online privacy indicated a desire for more government regulation; 82 percent agreed with the statement: "The government needs to step in and regulate how companies can use personal information." In addition, 92 percent of the households polled do not trust companies to keep personal information private, no matter what they promise.

Another consumer survey, conducted by the Pew Research Center for People and the Press in August 2000, found that 86 percent of Internet users favored opt-in privacy policies. Fifty-four percent said that tracking website users via "cookies" and other methods invades privacy. Ninety-four percent said that a company that violates its privacy policy should be sanctioned. Sixty-eight percent were concerned about hackers getting their credit card numbers.

Another indication of public feelings about privacy of personal information is the strong response to an alleged breach of privacy. In September 1996, a computer database called P-TRAK, operated by Lexis-Nexus to provide information to lawyers to use when locating heirs, litigants, and persons related to a case, raised a privacy issue furor on the Internet. Postings claimed the database was being used to identify individuals by name, social security number, mother's maiden name, and other personal information. Lexis-Nexis said it was releasing only names, addresses, telephone numbers, and, sometimes, maiden names.

When the press revealed that the Maryland Motor Vehicle Administration was selling license records to marketers, thousands of drivers took advantage of an opt-out provision that keeps their names off mailing lists. The outrage over whether social security numbers and other sensitive personal information is being divulged for commercial purposes was a surprise even to many privacy experts.

The public is increasingly aware of a right to privacy and is not hesitant about expressing anger at organizations responsible for violations. Legal developments over the last 100 years have also established privacy as a constitutional and common law right. The U.S. Supreme Court has described the origin of the right of privacy: "In a line of decisions . . . the Court has recognized that a right of personal privacy, or a guarantee of certain areas or zones of privacy, does exist under the Constitution" (*Roe v. Wade,* 1973). Some common law legal concepts that apply to privacy are intrusion upon seclusion (the right to be let alone), public disclosure of private facts, publicly placing a person in a false light, and appropriation of an employee's name and likeness.

PROPOSED PRIVACY LEGISLATION AND LEGAL DECISIONS

Federal and state governments have often stepped in to protect personal privacy by passing more laws. Recent legislation centers around the common law concept of public disclosure of private facts. "Private facts" are information about a person's medical history and condition, financial status, and family members, including children.

Proposed Legislation and Standards

During the 106th Congress a number of bills related to Internet privacy were introduced. Selected bills are described briefly here:

- The Consumer Internet Privacy Protection Act (H.R. 313) prohibits a computer service from disclosing to a third party any personally identifiable information about a subscriber without the subscriber's informed, written consent.

- The Social Security Online Privacy Protection Act (H.R. 367) prohibits a computer service from disclosing to a third party a subscriber's social security number without the subscriber's prior informed, written consent.

- The Online Privacy Protection Act (S. 809) requires a website or online service provider to provide an individual with a process to consent to or limit the disclosure of personal information collected by the service.

- The Electronic Rights for the 21st Century Act (S. 854) requires that a computer service provider disclose the contents of any subscriber's electronic communication to a governmental entity *only* in response to a warrant or a grand jury or trial subpoena.

- The Online Privacy Protection Act of 2000 (H.R. 3560) requires a website operator to inform consumers when personal information is being collected about them and provide a process for consumers to opt out of the collection/sharing program.

The Federal Trade Commission's task force on Internet privacy issued its report, *Fair Information Practices in the Electronic Marketplace,* to Congress on May 22, 2000. The report covered the broad issue of whether and how websites should be required to give consumers access to the personal data collected about them and shared with marketers. Another issue was mandating "a basic level of privacy protection for consumer-oriented commercial websites." The standards would cover notification to consumers about the use of personal data, an opt-out choice for consumers on the use of such information, the right of individuals to review personal information about them, restrictions on third-party access, and security measures to prevent unauthorized disclosure. The FTC found that only one in ten websites that collected consumer information had an industry privacy seal. Although the privacy seal was originally intended to be a simple industry "good practice" notice, it has evolved into an official statement from a third-party auditing firm attesting that the firm has audited the site's stated privacy policy.

Website Privacy Seals and Standards

WebTrust is a privacy seal developed in 1998 by the American Institute of Certified Public Accountants (AICPA). The privacy seal is granted to a company's website if its privacy practices and controls reveal the following:

- The specific kinds of information collected and used and any uses by third parties.

- How private information is collected online and used by the company.

- What happens if a consumer refuses to give private information.

- How private information is revised and corrected.

- How website information tracking devices are used and how the consumer may refuse to accept such a device.

- The security measures to ensure privacy of consumer's information.

The Open Profiling Standard (OPS) provides a voluntary framework covering the collection and sharing of personal information supplied by consumers visiting sites on the Web while assuring their privacy. The Web user receives a common electronic form for listing personal information, such as marital status, home ownership, hobbies, and other relevant marketing-related information. Users are notified when a website requests personal information. Users can give the site some or all of their personal information. The website must obtain the users' consent to give any personal information to another business or site.

The Platform for Privacy Preferences (P3) 1999 is a broader standard than OPS and would create a common set of computer codes that allow a website to transmit its privacy policies to a user's browser software. The user can then use the browser to communicate with websites that meet the user's criteria for privacy. Currently, sites often use "cookies" that can be read from or written to a user's hard drive. Data collection software routines and these cookie files stored on a user's computer can reveal the names of websites recently visited and activities during a visit, such as a transaction. The World-Wide Web Consortium (W3C), which has a 170-company membership, put together the P3 privacy initiative with the same goal as the Open Profiling Standard. W3C members Netscape and Microsoft will have browsers that will support P3.

TRUSTe, a nonprofit group backed by Netscape, IBM, and AT&T, proposes a sort of licensing and branding/logo system ("trustmarks") for website owners that will inform consumers of the website's privacy policies and practices. Those practices will be audited. Trustmarks would appear as icon buttons on licensed websites. A website would tell users how information about them would be used. Messages such as "no personally identifiable information collected" ("No Exchange"), "personal information collected is only used by the company/owner" (One-to-One Exchange), or "personal information gathered is sold to marketers or other third party only with the consumer's consent" (Third-Party Exchange) would be displayed. Users/consumers have a choice of what, if any, personal information to give the website. TRUSTe's audits of licensed websites would be done by a major accounting firm. TRUSTe's contracting, licensing, and logos will be backed by court actions if necessary.

U.S. Supreme Court Upholds Privacy Legislation

On January 12, 2000, the Supreme Court, in *Reno v. Condon,* upheld the Drivers Privacy Protection Act, which prohibits states from selling the personal information collected from licensed drivers and car owners. The states had been selling this personal information, including the person's picture on the license, to private investigators, direct marketers, and others. South Carolina had challenged the law, claiming that it infringed a state's right to regulate driving. The Supreme Court said the law "did not run afoul of the federalism principles" and that the act "regulates the states as owners of databases."

CONSUMERS STRIKE BACK

Consumer responses to recent breaches of privacy or attempts by companies to build massive databases of consumer information have been swift and highly negative. Most consumers are probably happy with the benefits of online shopping and are not that concerned about privacy. Nevertheless, e-commerce companies should be concerned about the relationship between Internet/Web privacy and security and consumer confidence, trust, and loyalty. There is a growing awareness among consumers that personal privacy encompasses the right to restrict and control personal information against commercial interests.

Infomediaries

Sick of being interrogated at a website about personal information: your name; home address; home phone, cell phone, pager, office, and e-mail numbers; buying habits; and future purchases? Why not ask to get paid for all this information, such as every time your name is rented for an e-mail ad mailing or for an ad hit on the website? After all, the website owner is getting paid.

The idea of consumer pay for information was suggested by John Hagel in an article in the January/February 1997 issue of *Harvard Business Review*. Hagel proposed setting up an information agent or broker (an "infomediary") for consumers to get money, coupons, discounts, or gifts in exchange for personal data. Hagel's idea is one way to solve the privacy versus profit conflict between website advertisers and consumers. An infomediary would also act as custodian for information captured on consumers; based on the privacy preferences of an individual, the infomediary would broker that information accordingly. The idea is similar to that of a mailing list broker for direct mail.

Reading a Privacy Policy

When deciding whether to use a website, consumers should evaluate the privacy policy carefully, keeping the following questions in mind:

❑ Does the privacy policy/agreement contain accurate descriptions of how personal information will be collected, maintained, manipulated, and shared?

❑ Is how the collection and use of personal information explained clearly and completely?

❑ Are there easy-to-use software tools to give permission to use only the personal information the consumer wants to give out?

❑ Do a couple of clicks (an "I agree" via a click/statement) make a "clickwrap" the same as a "shrinkwrap" license/contract?

❑ Can the consumer read and understand the *entire* website privacy policy/agreement?

❑ Is the policy placed "in close proximity" to areas of the site where personal information is collected?

❑ Is the full text of the policy available online, and can it be printed out?

　　❑ Is the policy written in clear, nonlegal, plain English that can be understood by the average person?

　　❑ Are the typeface, type size, line length, and any other graphic elements designed to make the policy readable, or is the policy presented in "mouse type" (a 5- or 6-point type size or smaller), which is common to documents meant to obfuscate any attempt at legibility and understanding?

❑ Does the policy accurately reflect the personal information collection techniques and usage currently practiced by the organization?

❑ Does the organization have its website policy and practices audited by an outside auditing firm?

Information Privacy Products

Consumers can also turn to a number of products and services designed to bypass a website's cookie-creating and information-gathering system. Zero-Knowledge Systems, a Montreal company, has a software product called Freedom that gives a user five digital pseudonyms to use on the Freedom system. Freedom encrypts Web browsing requests and sends them through at least three routers before reaching a final destination. Each message has three layers of encryption, with one layer taken off at each router, which learns where to send the message next. The source of the message and its final destination thus can be very difficult to uncover and match up. Other companies that have similar privacy protection products are Anonymizer.com, Hush Communications, PrivacyX, PrivaSeek, Enonymous, Network Associates, and ZipLip.

PRIVACY, LOYALTY, AND TRUST IN BUSINESS-TO-BUSINESS AND BUSINESS-TO-CONSUMER MARKETING

Privacy and security are vital to the creation of trust and confidence in a website. This holds true whether the website operates for business-to-consumer or business-to-business. Website operators must protect the confidentiality of information gathered on site visitors, consider consumers' expectations of privacy, and recognize a growing conflict with personal information gatherers.

In business-to-business marketing we find the same interrelationships among trust, reputation, loyalty, privacy/confidentiality, and security. *Trust building* involves privacy and security of transactions and confidential information. *Trust infrastructure, trusted transactions,* and *digital trust* are based on the security technologies of digital signatures, biometrics, encryption, intrusion detection of servers, firewalls, and access controls. Site security and soft assets protection of confidential proprietary information are also important. These concepts are discussed in the chapters on compliance, security, and protection of proprietary in formation.

Most successful and profitable businesses have a base of loyal customers, and much of this loyalty is based on trust. Consumer privacy protection is vital to the creation of trust, loyalty, and confidence in a business; together they enhance its reputation. As online alliances proliferate in the global economy, companies will increasingly form many new relationships with suppliers, affiliates, and former competitors or through e-business networks or similiar associations. Corporate reputations will increasingly be tied to these alliance partners.

E-business companies have had huge up-front acquisition costs for advertising, primarily for brand and name recognition. In many cases this has been a failure, resulting in no name recognition and no money left to run the business or service customers properly. Other companies have managed to get over the cost hurdle and settle in to do business on the Internet. But the more high tech the business environment becomes, the harder it is to build trusting customer relationships that can lead to long-term profits. The Internet is used mostly by Web surfers, making for lots of website "hits" but not loyal customers.

In *The Loyalty Effect* (1996), Frederick Reichheld set out a model of loyalty economics. Reichheld's core idea is that companies that cultivate loyal customers, employees, and shareholders consistently outperform the competition. Having a loyalty-based advantage means that customer loyalty and retention result in superior profit and growth. Conversely, emphasizing short-term earnings leads only to cost controls and reductions. According to Reichheld, it all starts with earning a customer's trust.

Reichheld looks to the creation of value to the customer, with loyalty "inextricably linked to the creation of value as both a cause and an effect." As an effect, loyalty measures the delivery of superior value by the company, such as repeat customers. As a cause, loyalty sets off a series of economic effects, such as revenue and market share growth, employee retention, productivity increases, and loyal investors. Reichheld's concept of "loyalty economics" is crucial to e-business seeking to create and hold consumer trust.

E-COMMERCE PRIVACY PRINCIPLES AND POLICY

Websites and the Internet have great potential for raising privacy liability risks. A conflict between the site operator and the user is almost inevitable because a key reason for a business to have a website is to market its products or services, whereas a key reason a person visits a particular website is to examine its marketing information. When marketer and consumer meet, the dynamics of information exchange occur and privacy problems may take shape. The website business usually desires as much information on a current or potential customer as it can get. The business may obtain information openly, by asking, or surreptitiously, through the use of techniques that use the information residing on the customer's computer.

Website operators need to be aware of potential privacy problems that can cause legal liabilities, as well as very bad publicity. Businesses gather information on site visitors by using cookies or other browser features that allow information to be read off or written to a computer's hard drive. Cookies are a means for website operators to obtain and store information about their users and to use that information for various marketing purposes. Users often do not know about this method of information gathering.

A customer may, of course, give information to the website business freely and without caring what the business does with it. On the other hand, before giving out personal, marketing-relevant information, the customer may want something in exchange and may want to know exactly how personal information is going to be used.

The trick for a website business is to turn privacy concerns into a business plus, rather than a minus. Handling privacy concerns effectively may also have a long-term benefit for all website owners: It may hold off more restrictive laws and government regulation on how business can be conducted on the Web.

PRIVACY PROTECTION POLICIES AND PRACTICES

An effective privacy protection policy should have three concurrent objectives:

1. **To minimize intrusiveness:** Create a proper balance between what an individual is expected to divulge to a company or website owner and what the individual seeks in return. The company should explain its information needs, collection practices, and information controls and security.

2. **To maximize fairness:** Give individuals a right of access to their records and information for reviewing, copying, and correcting.

3. **To create a legally enforceable expectation of privacy:** Develop and define obligations regarding uses and disclosures that will be made of collected and recorded information about an individual. Restrict the website operator's or recordkeeper's discretion to voluntarily disclose information about an individual.

PRINCIPLES OF PRIVACY AND INFORMATION PROTECTION

The following principles should guide website operators' collection and use of private information:

1. Don't collect information unless its need and relevance have been clearly established.

2. Don't collect information fraudulently or unfairly.

3. Use information only if it is accurate and current.

4. Individuals have the right to know of information stored about them, why it has been recorded, and how it is collected, used, and disseminated, as well as the right to examine that information upon request.

5. Provide a clear procedure on how the individual can correct, delete, or amend inaccurate, obsolete, or irrelevant information.

6. Ensure the reliability, integrity, and availability of collected, maintained, used, or disseminated personal information and take precautions to prevent its misuse.

7. Provide a clear procedure and safeguards to prevent personal information collected for one purpose from being used for another purpose or disclosed to a third party without an individual's consent. Also provide a right to notification of disclosure of information.

8. Federal, state, and local governments should collect only legally authorized personal information.

Since 1974, federal and state laws have incorporated these principles of privacy protection. Most laws cover individuals' right to see and copy information collected about them, correct or amend such information, and seek redress of grievances or injury caused them as a consequence of the use of inaccurate data. Recordkeeping organizations must always be concerned that their information is up-to-date, complete, and secure. Data collection, dissemination, and security are all important. Organizations are responsible for verifying data they collect and for correcting any false information they knowingly pass on to another party. Organizations cannot argue a general presumption of accuracy regarding third-party data they use or transmit as a legal defense.

WEBSITE OPERATOR'S PRIVACY ASSESSMENT CHECKLIST

The following checklist should be used to assess a website's compliance with privacy protection requirements:

❑ Does your site collect personal information from site visitors through cookie files or electronic registration forms?

❑ How does your site use a visitor's personal information?

    ❑ What kinds of information are collected about site visitors?

    ❑ How will this information be used, and is there a user consent form covering company and third-party use of the information?

    ❑ Can visitors opt in or opt out of your marketing database or mailing list?

    ❑ Is the information current and accurate for its intended use?

    ❑ Can visitors look at, change, or delete any collected personal information?

    ❑ Do you describe the kinds of legal actions that would force the release of personal information to a third party?

❑ Does your site have a visitor's personal information privacy policy?

❑ Is your privacy policy or information disclosure notice posted on your website?

❑ Are your information privacy practices audited by an independent third party, such as an accounting firm, and are the results of the audit available to the website user?

2

A PRIMER ON PRIVACY LAW

Before you can devise fair and effective employee or consumer privacy policies and security measures, you need to have a working knowledge of privacy-related laws. You also need to know that these laws are a patchwork of common, federal, and state laws that are constantly evolving.

PRIVACY AS A CONSTITUTIONAL RIGHT

The concept of a personal right to privacy can be traced to an 1890 article in the *Harvard Law Review* by Samuel D. Warren and Louis D. Brandeis. They advanced the idea that there existed enough case law for recognition of a formal legal right of privacy. They argued that the "right to be let alone" was self-evident, and referred to the "precincts of private and domestic life" as sacred. Fifteen years later, the Georgia Supreme Court ruled that a man named Pavesich could recover damages from an insurance company that had used a picture of him in an advertisement and testimonial without his permission (1905).

In a 1965 case, *Griswold v. Connecticut*, the U.S. Supreme Court struck down a Connecticut law forbidding the use of contraceptives by married couples. In *Eisenstadt v. Baird*, the Supreme Court removed a ban on the distribution of contraceptives even to unmarried couples. Personal privacy had overruled state law.

Expanding the concept further, in *Roe v. Wade* (1973) the Supreme Court found that the "right of privacy . . . is broad enough to encompass a woman's decision whether or not to terminate her pregnancy." The Court went on to describe the origin of the right of privacy:

> In a line of decisions . . . the Court has recognized that a right of personal privacy, or a guarantee of certain areas or zones of privacy, does exist under the Constitution. In various contexts, the Courts or individual Justices have, indeed, found at least the roots of that right in the First Amendment . . . ; in the Fourth and Fifth Amendments. . . ; in the penumbras of the Bill of Rights . . . ; in the Ninth Amendment . . . ; or in the concept of liberty guaranteed by the first section of the Fourteenth Amendment.

COMMON LAW CONCEPTS OF PRIVACY

The development of a common law right to privacy and of a privacy invasion tort is described in the *Restatement (Second) of Torts,* Section 652B (1977), as follows: "One who intentionally intrudes, physically or otherwise, upon the solitude or seclusion of another, or his personal affairs or concerns, is subject to liability to the other for invasion of his privacy, if the intrusion would be highly offensive to the ordinary reasonable person." As mentioned in Chapter 1, the four common law legal concepts that apply to privacy are (1) intrusion upon seclusion (the right to be let alone), (2) public disclosure of private facts, (3) publicity placing a person in a false light, and (4) appropriation of an employee's name and likeness.

Proving *wrongful disclosure* of private or embarrassing facts usually requires that the information have been communicated to more than one person. However, any disclosure of false information could lead to a defamation suit. Defamation can be via writing (libel) or speech (slander). Both are communications of false information to a third party that injures someone's reputation. Other elements of defamation are the reasonable identification of the defamed person and damage to reputation. If the defamation refers to a public figure or is a matter of public concern, it must be proved that the defamatory language was false and that it was communicated knowingly or with a reckless disregard for the truth or falsity of the information.

FEDERAL LAWS AFFECTING PRIVACY AND SECURITY

Many federal laws and regulations affect individual privacy, security, and e-business. A number of them are discussed in this section. It is important to note that:

- Most federal laws apply to employers with 15 or more employees.

- Under antidiscrimination laws, discrimination does not have to be intentional for an employer, or his or her agent, to be in violation of the law.

- Every legislative act has been followed by many, and often conflicting, regulations and rulings from administrative agencies, as well as court decisions.

- Laws are usually never clarified for years; that is, it takes a build-up of case law before a law's full intent and substance are revealed.

Code of Fair Information Practices and the Privacy Act of 1974

When Congress examined the issue of privacy in the early 1970s, there was a growing public awareness of actual and potential abuses of personal privacy, particularly in the area of information gathering and dissemination by public agencies and private companies, such as commercial credit bureaus. In 1973, the Department of Health, Education and Welfare developed the Code of Fair Information Practices to govern the collection and use of information by the federal government. The principles of the code were incorporated in the Privacy Act of 1974 (Public Law 93-579).

In 1974, Congress passed the first federal legislation providing privacy protection. The Privacy Act of 1974 covered federal agencies and government contractors performing recordkeeping functions on behalf of a federal agency. Federal agencies were required to provide safeguards for an individual against an invasion of personal privacy. Unless exempted by law, federal agencies were required to

1. permit an individual to determine what records about him or her are collected, maintained, used, or disseminated by such agencies;

2. allow an individual to prevent his or her records from being used by other agencies without his or her consent;

3. allow an individual access to his or her records, to copy, correct, and amend them;

4. collect, maintain, use, or disseminate any record of identifiable personal information *only* for necessary or lawful purposes and ensure that the information is current and accurate for its intended use;

5. make exceptions to the act's requirements only where specific statutory authority exists; and

6. be subject to civil suit for violations of an individual's privacy rights and damages for willful or intentional acts.

Age Discrimination in Employment Act (ADEA) of 1967

The ADEA (29 U.S.C. 621 et seq. (1967)) prohibits discrimination on the basis of age. Employers' inquiries about age have been considered evidence of discrimination against applicants in protected age groups, from 40 to 65 years of age. The act covers hiring, referral, classification, and other conditions of employment. Firms with 25 or more employees fall under the act. The administrative agency is the Department of Labor.

Cable Communications Policy Act of 1984

This legislation (47 U.S.C. 55) protects the privacy of cable television subscriber records.

Cable Act of 1992

Under this act (47 U.S.C. 521), privacy protections enacted in 1984 were extended to cable companies that provide cellular and other wireless services. Companies are required to inform subscribers of the nature of personally identifiable customer information collected and how that information is used. Disclosure to third parties requires customer consent. (There are some exceptions to this requirement.)

Communications Assistance for Law Enforcement Act (CALEA) of 1994

CALEA (Public Law 103-414; 47 U.S.C. 1001-1010) will facilitate law enforcement agency surveillance in digital, wireless, cellular, and other advanced communications technologies and services. The law requires telecommunications carriers to assist the lawful interception needs of law enforcement agencies. CALEA also requires common carriers and telecommunications manufacturers to provide the necessary equipment to meet the technical assistance needs of the FBI and other law enforcement agencies to carry out electronic surveillance. This assistance is to be accomplished while protecting the privacy of communications and without impeding the introduction of new technologies and services.

CALEA requires telecommunications carriers to ensure that their systems can isolate expeditiously the content of targeted communications and information, identifying its origin and destination; provide this information to law enforcement agencies so it can be retransmitted; and carry out intercepts unobtrusively, so targets are not made aware of the interception, and in a manner that does not violate the privacy and security of other communications.

Communications Decency Act of 1996

This act (Public Law 104-104) extends the Communications Act of 1934 to cover all telecommunications equipment, including faxes and e-mail, and makes it a federal crime to use this equipment to annoy, abuse, threaten, or harass the contacted party. The act also has penalties for any parties, including employers, who knowingly allow the use of telecommunications equipment under their control for any of the listed activities.

Computer Security Act of 1987

This law (Public Law 104-106) provides for the security and privacy of sensitive information in federal computer systems through the development of security standards, research, and training, and the establishment of computer security plans by all systems operators. The act also provides for a federal Privacy Advisory Board.

Computer Matching and Privacy Protection Act of 1988

This act (Public Law 100-503) targets computer matching programs conducted by federal agencies, in which computerized information from two databases is automatically compared to detect common individuals or discrepancies in records. Many government databases contain sensitive personal information. The act established agency data integrity boards to review, approve, and monitor matching programs.

Debt Collection Act of 1982

The Debt Collection Act (Public Law 104-134) established restrictions on the release of federal debt information to private credit bureaus.

Driver's Privacy Protection Act of 1994

This act (Public Law 104-294) prohibits the use of state motor vehicle lists by parties other than government agencies, law enforcement agencies, and the judicial system. Statistical market researchers may have access and use lists "so long as the personal information is not published, redisclosed, or used to contact individuals." State motor vehicle agencies "shall not knowingly disclose or make available to any person or entity personal information about any individual obtained by the department in connection with a motor vehicle record."

The act requires an opt-out opportunity for drivers, meaning that states must offer a way for drivers to indicate that they do not want their names on mailing lists. Under the act, an individual may sue a state motor vehicle department for giving out personal information and any firm that uses such information without the individual's specific permission.

On January 12, 2000, the Supreme Court, in *Reno v. Condon*, upheld the Drivers Privacy Protection Act. The states had been selling personal information, including the person's picture on the driver's license, to private investigators, direct marketers, and others. South Carolina had challenged the law, claiming that it infringed on a state's right to regulate driving. The Supreme Court said the law "did not run afoul of the federalism principles" and that the act "regulates the states as owners of databases."

Electronic Communications Privacy Act of 1986

The federal electronic surveillance statutes were originally enacted as Title III of the Omnibus Crime Control and Safe Streets Act of 1968. They were amended by the Electronic Communications Privacy Act of 1986 (ECPA; Public Law 99-508, 18 U.S.C. Sec. 2510-2520 and 2701-2710). ECPA extends the protection of the Wiretap Act of 1968 to electronic communications and communications systems, including radio, satellite, and data communications.

27

Excluded from coverage are any radio transmission "readily accessible to the general public" and certain types of protected radio signals.

The ECPA protects the privacy of transmitted and stored electronic communications from interception and disclosure. It covers electronic communications made by "any transfer of signs, signals, writings, images, sounds, data or intelligence of any nature transmitted in whole or in part by a wire, radio, electromagnetic, photoelectronic or photo-optical system that affects interstate or foreign commerce." The only requirement of the act is that the information affect interstate or foreign commerce. The ECPA applies to government, private, and public systems, exempting those systems that have no expectation of privacy, such as communications made through a tone-only paging device, a tracking device, or the radio portion of a cordless telephone communication.

Under the ECPA it is illegal to intercept electronic communications or to use or disclose the contents of electronic communications to another person; this is a felony carrying fines and prison terms. The person whose communication was intercepted can bring suit in federal court. Penalties are greater when the interception was for commercial advantage or illegal purpose, and the plaintiff may recover actual damages and profits made as a result of the violation.

The privacy of electronic mail is protected under the law, with a misdemeanor penalty for those who break into an electronic communications system holding messages. The ECPA covers any service "which provides to users thereof the ability to send or receive wire or electronic communications." Remote computing services (systems that provide public computer communications storage or processing) are covered, as well as "any person or entity providing the wire or electronic communication service." A key required element is that the system be configured for privacy. Offenses committed for commercial advantage or malicious destruction or damage carry a fine of up to $250,000, a one-year prison term, or both.

For both stored and transmitted communications, the intent standard applies to any defendant. It must be proven that the defendant intentionally sought to intercept, alter, damage, or destroy the data communication or message. It is illegal for providers of electronic communications services to the public to knowingly divulge the contents of any communication except to the sender or intended recipient of the information.

Wiretap Authority   Under the ECPA, law enforcement agencies seeking to use wiretaps must obtain the approval of certain high-level Justice Department officials, then a court order authorizing or approving their proposed interception. The provisions of Title III specifically assign review powers to the attorney general but allow this authority to be delegated to other Justice Department officials. The Department of Justice (DOJ) review process

> must occur prior to the submission to the court of an application for interception. Such review and approval must, in almost all instances, precede the actual interception. However, in certain "emergency" situations, interception may temporarily precede application to the court. In those instances, the Department's authorization must still be obtained prior to interception, and the application to the court must be submitted within 48 hours of the interception.

Applications for electronic surveillance are initially reviewed by the Electronic Surveillance Unit of the Criminal Division's Office of Enforcement Operations.

An important restriction on the use of electronic surveillance by law enforcement officials is the requirement that the government obtain an order from a court of competent jurisdiction prior to the use of most types of electronic surveillance. A "court of competent jurisdiction" is defined as (18 U.S.C. 3127(2))

> (A) a district court of the United States (including a magistrate [United States magistrate judge] of such a court) or a United States Court of Appeals; or

> (B) a court of general criminal jurisdiction of a State authorized by the law of that State to enter orders authorizing the use of pen register or a trap and trace device.

As noted above, the ECPA broadened the definition of *communications* to include electronic communications, including computers, fax machines, and paging devices.

The application for electronic surveillance must be specific enough for the court to conclude

1. that probable cause exists that the listed persons have committed, are committing, or will commit offenses that are proper predicates for the specific type of electronic surveillance;

2. that probable cause exists that all or some of these persons have used, are using, or will use a targeted facility or targeted premises in connection with the commission of predicate offenses (under Title III of the ECPA); and

3. that probable cause exists that the targeted facility has been used, is being used, or will be used in connection with the predicate offenses.

The court application must also contain: "a complete statement as to other investigative procedures that have been tried and failed, or reasonably appear unlikely to succeed if tried, or which would be too dangerous to employ, and a complete statement of all other applications for electronic surveillance involving the persons, facilities, or premises which are subject to the current application."

The ECPA authorizes applications for the "roving interception" of wire communications: "An application for the interception of wire communications without specifying the facility or facilities to be targeted may be made in those instances where it can be shown that the subject or subjects of the interception have demonstrated a purpose to thwart interception by changing facilities." ECPA also contains a provision authorizing an emergency interception of electronic communications before a court authorization can be obtained, as long as

> such officer is specifically designated, prior to the interception, by the Attorney General, Deputy Attorney General, or Associate Attorney General and where an emergency situation exists that involves (1) immediate danger of death or se-

rious bodily injury to any person, (2) conspiratorial activities threatening the national security interest, or (3) conspiratorial activities characteristic of organized crime. The statute requires that grounds must exist under which an order could be entered to authorize the interception and that an application be made within 48 hours after the interception has occurred or begins to occur. If a court order is obtained within that time frame, the interception may continue as ordered.

If the application is denied, the contents of the interception must be treated as a violation of Title III, and an inventory of the interception must be given to the party named in the application.

Stored Electronic Communications ECPA protection extends to electronic communications stored after transmission. Requirements for government access are set forth in 18 U.S.C. 2703-2705: a search warrant issued under the Federal Rules of Criminal Procedure (Rule 41, search and seizure) or equivalent state warrant. The government can also use an administrative subpoena authorized by a federal or state statute or a federal or state grand jury or trial subpoena. Another avenue is via a court order for disclosure, if the government can show "there is reason to believe the contents of a wire or electronic communication, or the records or other information sought, are relevant to a legitimate law enforcement inquiry."

In *Steve Jackson Games v. United States Secret Service* (1994), SJG filed a civil suit in federal court against the Secret Service under Title I of the ECPA. A federal district court had found that the Secret Service violated Title II of the ECPA by seizing stored electronic communications (e-mail) in SJG's computers without complying with statutory provisions. The district court did not find that the Secret Service "intercepted" the e-mail in violation of Title I.

The issue that came before the U.S. Court of Appeals for the Fifth Circuit was the definition of *interception*; specifically, the seizure of a computer on which is stored private e-mail that has been sent to an electronic bulletin board but has not yet been read by the recipients. Section 2511(1)(a) of the ECPA prohibits "intentionally intercepting . . . any wire, oral, or electronic communications" unless authorized by court order. Section 2520 allows those whose electronic communications are intercepted to bring a civil suit for damages.

In ECPA, *intercept* is defined as "the aural or other acquisition of the contents of any wire, electronic, or oral communication through the use of any electronic, mechanical, or other device." SJG argued that the e-mail could still be intercepted under the ECPA even though it was not in transit and argued that it was the intent of Congress to protect e-mail and bulletin boards.

The appeals court ruled that the

> language of the Act [Title I] controls . . . electronic storage is defined as any temporary, intermediate storage of a wire or electronic communication incidental to the electronic transmission thereof. . . . The E-mail in issue was in "electronic storage." Congress' use of the word "transfer" in the definition of "electronic communication," and its omission in that definition of the phrase "any electronic storage of such communication" reflects that Congress did not intend for "intercept" to apply to electronic communications in storage. . . . We find no indication in either the act or its legislative history that Congress intended for conduct that is clearly prohibited by Title II to furnish the basis for a civil remedy under Title I as well.

The ECPA was updated to clarify electronic communications in storage, create new offences, and set punishments (18 U.S.C., Sec. 2701).

Employee Polygraph Protection Act of 1988

This act (Public Law 104-201; 29 U.S.C. 20001-20008) prohibits the use of lie detectors or any similar device "for the purpose of rendering a diagnostic opinion regarding the honesty of an individual." "Lie detectors" include polygraph, deceptograph, voice stress analyzer, psychological stress evaluator, or "any similar device for the purpose of rendering a diagnostic opinion regarding the honesty or dishonesty of an individual." Under the act, it is illegal to

1. make any employee or prospective employee take a lie detector test;

2. use or get the results of any lie detector test of an employee; and

3. discharge or take disciplinary action or discriminate against any current or prospective employee who refuses to take a lie detector test, who fails a lie detector test, or who files a complaint under this law.

The law lays out the rights of the examinee, how the test should be conducted, qualifications and requirements of examiners, and disclosure of test results.

Violations of this law carry a civil penalty of not more than $10,000. However, the employer is open to civil actions by the employee and may be liable for back pay and benefits, court costs, and attorney's fees. The statute of limitations is three years after the date of the alleged violation.

This law exempts a number of parties, including:

- government employees;

- Defense Department contractors and consultants;

- intelligence or counterintelligence personnel, consultants, or contractors; and

- firms and agencies involved in ongoing investigations, as long as the employee is thought to be involved in an economic crime, and the employer details in a statement to the examinee the reasons for the test. To be regarded as an "ongoing investigation," the investigation must deal with a specific incident, and an "economic loss or injury" must have occurred. An investigation cannot be part of a sustained surveillance program, and the loss must have happened and be documented via report, audit, or initial incident investigation. The economic loss could result from theft, embezzlement, fraud, or industrial espionage or sabotage. Employees who had access to the property under investigation and of whom the employer has a "reasonable suspicion" may be subject to lie detector/polygraph testing.

There is also a limited exemption for private security services that use armored cars, alarm security systems installers, utilities, public transportation, currency and precious commodities handlers, and controlled substance manufacturers or distributors.

An individual conducting polygraph testing must have a valid and current state license and be bonded. Note that the burden is on the employer to show that all the various elements exist to conduct polygraph tests. Thus, employers are urged to consult with legal counsel prior to using lie detection testing.

Equal Employment Opportunity Act of 1972

The Equal Employment Opportunity Commission (EEOC), which administers the act (42 U.S.C. 2000 et seq.), issued guidelines relating to any selection techniques that may be improperly used to discriminate illegally against racial, ethnic, religious, age, or sex groups. EEOC guidelines require that any employment selection procedure be supported by validity and by evidence of "a high degree of utility."

Fair Credit Reporting Act (FCRA) of 1970

FCRA (Public Law 91–508; 15 U.S.C. 1681 et seq.) regulates methods of obtaining credit information about an applicant or an employee. Essentially, the law requires that an applicant be informed in writing that a credit report is being sought, and the information sought must be defined. Under FCRA, a credit bureau may furnish an employer with a report for "employment purposes," defined as a report used for the purpose of evaluation only. Section 615 of FCRA requires that if the report user denies employment to an individual based wholly or partly on information in the report, he or she must advise the individual and give that person the name of the credit agency that made the report.

A bill to shore up the savings and loan insurance fund was signed into law on September 30, 1996 (Public Law 104-208). One of its provisions modifies the Fair Credit Reporting Act of 1970, which governs credit bureaus and the compilation of individuals' credit histories. The law gives consumers new and more definite ways of correcting errors in credit reports. Consumers can get a free credit report after their credit history has been used to deny them credit for any class of transaction, such as insurance or employment. Information that causes adverse action must, upon written request from the consumer, be disclosed to the consumer within 60 days. Credit bureaus must delete disputed information if it cannot be verified.

The law also covers banks, retailers, and other businesses that supply credit bureaus with consumer information. These businesses must take steps to ensure the accuracy of the information collected and investigate disputed information. They can avoid liability if they can show "by a preponderance of the evidence that at the time of the alleged violation [they] maintained reasonable procedures to assure compliance" with the act's accuracy and privacy safeguards.

Affiliated companies can share consumer information for marketing purposes.

Family Educational Rights and Privacy Act of 1974

This act (Public Law 93-508) limits disclosure of educational records from schools and colleges that get federal funds.

Federal Contract Compliance Regulations (1968)

These regulations (Executive Order 11246 as amended by Executive Order 11375) prohibit discrimination on the basis of race, color, religion, sex, or national origin and require that employers take "affirmative action" to ensure equal opportunity provisions. These regulations apply to companies with federal contracts or subcontracts of more than $10,000.

Companies with over $50,000 in federal contracts and 50 or more employees are required to file affirmative action plans with the Office of Federal Contract Compliance.

Identity Theft and Assumption Deterrence Act of 1998

This act (Public Law 105–318) makes it a criminal offense for someone to knowingly transfer or use another person's means of identification, such as name, social security number, driver's license, passport number, date of birth, or any unique biometric-derived data, with the intent to commit any unlawful activity.

National Labor Relations Act (NLRA) of 1947

NLRA (29 U.S.C. 151 et seq.) covers unfair labor practices. The act established the National Labor Relations Board, which investigates and arbitrates charges of unfair labor practices, generally in the area of union organizing and an employer's attempts either to thwart union organizing attempts or influence an employee's actions regarding unions.

Occupational Safety and Health Act (OSHA) of 1970

OSHA (Public Law 105-197; 29 U.S.C. 651 et seq.) was originally created to protect workers from unsafe working conditions. Recently, however, OSHA has sought, through court action and rules, to allow workers and the agency broad access to employer records relating to workers' safety and health.

Privacy Act of 1974

This act (Public Law 93-579) restricts federal agencies from releasing personal information and allows an individual to review files kept about him or her by certain federal agencies.

Right to Financial Privacy Act of 1978

This law (Public Law 95-630) limits the access of law enforcement agencies to an individual's bank and financial records.

Telephone Consumer Protection Act of 1991

This act (Public Law 102-243) regulates the activities of telemarketers regarding time of calls, disclosure of marketer, and description and costs of the product or service.

Title VII, Civil Rights Act of 1964

Title VII defines *discrimination* in comprehensive terms as any employment practice that has an adverse impact on the members of any protected class. It should be noted that discrimination does not have to be intentional for the employer to be in violation of the law (see *Griggs v. Duke Power Co.*, 401 U.S. 424 (1971), 3 EDP, Section 8137). The Equal Employment Opportunity Commission (EEOC) was established as the administrative agency for Title VII.

Video Privacy Protection Act of 1988

This act (Public Law 100-618) protects the privacy of video rental records.

Omnibus Crime Control Act of 1994

Part of this legislation requires telephone company networks to meet the wiretapping needs of law enforcement agencies. Law enforcement officials cannot obtain e-mail addresses by subpoena. They also must get a court order to learn caller location of a cellular or wireless user.

Americans With Disabilities Act (ADA) of 1992

ADA (Public Law 104-1) requires that any health information obtained by employers be stored in segregated and secured personnel files and treated as confidential.

Employee Retirement Income Security Act (ERISA) of 1974

ERISA (Public Law 93-406, 88 Stat. 829) also affects personal privacy and security issues.

3

HEALTHCARE LAW MANDATES SECURITY AND PRIVACY

The privacy of health information has become a major concern. The federal government has passed legislation to deal with this issue. The Health Insurance Portability and Accountability Act (HIPPA) of 1996 (Public Law 104-191) aims to improve "the efficiency and effectiveness of the health care system by encouraging the development of a health information system through the establishment of standards and requirements for the electronic transmission of certain health information." HIPPA also calls for standards to protect the privacy of personal health information and preserve trust in the provider-physician-patient relationship.

The act defines *individually identifiable health information* as any information collected from an individual that relates to his or her past, present, or future physical or mental health or condition, as well as healthcare and payment provisions. Any information that identifies an individual or makes it possible to identify an individual is also included in that definition.

HEALTH INFORMATION PRIVACY RECOMMENDATIONS

In 1997 the secretary of health and human services developed detailed privacy standards for individual health information, addressing

- the rights of an individual to personally identifiable health information;

41

- procedures to exercise these rights; and
- the authorized uses and disclosures of such information.

PROPOSED INFORMATION STANDARDS

Standards for handling individually identifiable health information were published in the *Federal Register* on November 11, 1999. They apply to health plans, healthcare clearinghouses, and healthcare providers (called covered entities) that keep or transmit health information in electronic form or paper printouts. The standards affect every company with a health plan or an onsite health facility. Business partners of providers are also covered by the privacy and security provisions.

The standards apply to financial and administrative data elements and transactions. There is a standard for a unique health identifier for each individual, employer, health plan, and healthcare provider and the purposes for which the identifier may be used. Security standards cover the costs of security measures; the extent of training needed; the value of audit trails in computerized record systems; the needs and capabilities of small and rural healthcare providers; and ensuring that a healthcare clearinghouse has adequate security policies and procedures.

Under HIPPA, any person or organization that maintains or transmits health information must "maintain reasonable and appropriate administrative, technical, and physical safeguards" that will

- ensure the integrity and confidentiality of the information,
- protect against "any reasonably anticipated" threat or hazard to security and integrity of the information,
- prevent unauthorized uses or disclosures of the information, and
- ensure compliance by officers and employees with the safeguards.

PROPOSED INFORMATION STANDARDS

The announced standards include the following:

- With a few exceptions, protected health information should be disclosed only for the purpose of healthcare, and "no more than is necessary to accomplish the intended purpose of the use or disclosure." Exceptions include promoting public health and research, a program exception or one made by the enrollee or with the enrollee's permission, or for audits or law enforcement. Again, there should be no more than minimal disclosure, only what is necessary to accomplish the intended purpose for which the information is being disclosed.

- Patients must be able to view, amend, and correct their records, and find out who has had access to them. They should be able to restrict use to treatment, payment, or healthcare operations, as long as the requested restrictions are agreed to by the healthcare provider.

- Employers who receive medical information in the process of reviewing claims cannot use the information to make employment-related decisions or for any other purpose unrelated to healthcare.

- Organizations that collect protected health information, such as hospitals, HMOs, and other covered healthcare providers, must take appropriate measures to safeguard all health information.

- Users and holders (e.g., insurance companies, business partners, claims processors) of health information must implement administrative, technical, and physical safeguards for the security of such information.

- Anyone who gains access to medical information in the course of doing business, such as insurers for the payment of claims, drug distributors, and billing service companies, must be held to the same standards of confidentiality and limits on disclosure as hospitals and covered entities. Protected healthcare information cannot be disclosed to a business partner without satisfactory assurance that it will be "appropriately safeguarded." *Satisfac-*

43

tory assurance requires a contract between the covered entity and the business partner covering how such information is to be used and safeguarded.

- Individuals or enrollees in a healthcare program must also have the right to know who uses or maintains their health information and for what purposes. Enrollees would have the right to inspect, copy, and amend or correct personal information. Enrollees or their representatives would have the right to get a written statement from the healthcare provider about the purposes for which such information may be used, disclosed, or accessed.

- Covered entities must have:

  1. a privacy official who is "responsible for the development and implementation of the privacy policies and procedures of the entity;"

  2. a contact person or office to receive complaints and provide further information;

  3. a training program to provide information on the entity's policies and procedures;

  4. appropriate administrative, technical, and physical safeguards and procedures to protect the privacy of health information;

  5. sanctions for violations of policies and procedures; and

  6. documentation of the entire compliance program: policies, procedures, personnel, training, safeguards, sanctions, auditing, and monitoring.

So far, HIPPA has not fleshed out privacy and security provisions for third-party liability, types of safeguards, and how an individual may refuse to have personal health information shared with third parties.

The Clinton administration issued the following health information privacy rules on December 20, 2000. They became effective on February 26, 2001:

PROPOSED INFORMATION STANDARDS

- Doctors, hospitals, pharmacies, and insurers must give patients a clear written notice of their rights, explaining how medical information will be stored, used, and disclosed. Every patient has the right to obtain a disclosure history, listing entities that received information unrelated to treatment or payment.

- Healthcare providers and health plans must have internal procedures to protect the privacy of medical information. They must also designate a privacy officer to help patients with questions and complaints. In addition, pro- viders must develop privacy policies and procedures and train their employees to guard the privacy of medical data.

- Doctors, hospitals, and health plans must ensure compliance with the new standards by business partners, affiliates, and third-party suppliers. If a violation is known and no steps are taken to correct it, a doctor or hospital can be held responsible for the violation.

- Doctors and hospitals must obtain written consent from patients before disclosing their medical information even for routine purposes like treatment or payment of claims. These consent forms have to be retained for a minimum of six years.

- The patient could sign one consent form, in the initial visit to a doctor, authorizing future disclosures for the same thing. Disclosures for other purposes could be made only if the patient gave separate, specific authorization. The patient may also revoke this consent.

- Personal medical information may not be disclosed for purposes unrelated to healthcare unless the patient explicitly gives permission. Consumers have a federal right to inspect and copy information in their medical records. They can also request correction of any information. Providers must keep track of everyone who has received medical information from the records; the patient can see this record.

The new privacy rules cover electronic records and their printouts, all paper records, and oral communications by health plans and providers.

The federal rules limit access to medical records by law enforcement; access now requires a warrant, subpoena, civil investigation demand, or administrative supoena issued by government investigators.

The disclosure of medical information is limited to the "minimum necessary" for any purpose, such as paying a bill. Doctors have discretion in determining how much information to disclose to another healthcare provider.

There are several privacy loopholes in the rules. First, pharmacies are permitted to share patients' prescription records with companies that want to send patients "educational materials." Foundations affiliated with hospitals can access patient information for fundraising. Other marketers will surely try to exploit the education route with infomercials and sales pitches.

These new rules do not supersede state privacy laws. The penalty for violating the federal healthcare privacy rules is a civil fine of $25,000; criminal violations carry a $50,000 fine and a year in prison. A person who violates the rules for personal gain or commercial advantage can be fined $250,000 and draw a prison sentence of up to 10 years.

PENALTIES FOR NONCOMPLIANCE AND VIOLATIONS

Anyone (including doctors and hospitals) who knowingly violates the confidentiality of a unique health identifier, obtains individually identifiable health information, or discloses such information to another person can be fined up to $50,000 and imprisoned for one year, or both. If the offense is committed under false pretenses, the maximum fine increases to $100,000 and the possible prison sentence goes up to five years. If the offense is committed with the intent to "sell, transfer, or use" the information for "commercial advantage, personal gain, or malicious harm," the fine jumps to a maximum of $250,000 and the prison sentence to not more than 10 years.

4

PRIVACY OF PERSONAL FINANCIAL INFORMATION

The Financial Services Modernization Act (FSMA) of 1999 is a comprehensive reform measure that allows banks, insurance companies, brokerages, and financial advisory services to merge or develop their own mix of financial services. It includes provisions for protecting personal financial information.

SCOPE OF FINANCIAL PRIVACY LAW AND REGULATIONS

FSMA defines *financial institution* broadly as "any institution which is engaged in financial activities under section 4(k) of the Bank Holding Company Act of 1956." Businesses engaging in financial activities normally include banking, insurance, and securities. However, the Federal Reserve Board, which has the authority to determine which activities are "financial," defines those activities as any that the Fed has determined to be so closely related to banking as to be a "proper incident thereto" and "engaging . . . in any activity that a bank or holding company may engage in" (see *Federal Register*, vol. 65, no. 41, March 1, 2000, pp. 11174–6). These broad definitions bring a multitude of businesses under the privacy provisions of the act.

The Federal Trade Commission (FTC) is responsible for regulating "other persons" who are not financial institutions but receive personal information from a financial institution and establish a customer relationship. The FTC has noted that "a relationship between such a business and a consumer is more than an isolated transaction." Examples of such businesses are mortgage brokerages and any entity that obtains credit for a customer.

Other businesses may be classified as financial institutions under the act depending on their involvement in financial activities that serve consumers. These businesses include accountants, tax preparation services, investment advisory services, retailers with credit cards, auto leasing companies, data processing services for financial information, and check cashers.

State insurance authorities are regulators of insurance companies and are charged with issuing privacy standards.

The privacy regulations apply only to consumers, defined as individuals who have a continuing relationship with a financial institution. Businesses that are not significantly engaged in financial activities are exempt from FSMA.

The privacy section of FSMA opens as follows:

> It is the policy of the Congress that each financial institution has an affirmative and continuing obligation to respect the privacy of its customers and to protect the security and confidentiality of those customers' non-public personal information.

This is a strong statement on privacy and signals Congress's interest in ensuring that consumers' personal information remains private.

By July 1, 2001, a financial institution must have in place privacy standards on the collection and use of consumers' nonpublic personal information. These standards and practices should be designed to

1. provide an initial notice to all customers about the institution's privacy policies and practices;

2. ensure the security and confidentiality of customer records and information;

3. protect against any anticipated threats or hazards to the security, integrity, and accuracy of such records; and

4. protect against unauthorized access to or use of such records or information that could result in substantial harm or inconvenience to any customer.

The privacy regulations require that financial institutions give three "clear and conspicuous" notices to customers/consumers:

1. An initial privacy notice when a customer relationship is established with the institution, describing the institution's privacy policies and practices.

2. An opt-out opportunity notice if the institution plans to share information with unaffiliated third parties or others and the customer wants to bar it.

3. An annual privacy notice, once every 12 months, for continuing customer relationships.

If a notice is in electronic form, such as on a Web page, it should be clear, prominent, and user-friendly, and appear on the website home page and in any area or linking pages where information is collected.

STATE LAWS ON FINANCIAL PRIVACY

FSMA does not affect state privacy laws. If a state law offers greater protection, a claimant may file an action under the state statute. This means that banks may have to comply with all state consumer privacy laws. States may adopt stronger privacy laws, such as requiring financial services to get written consent from consumers before sharing their personal financial information with affiliates or third parties.

PRIVACY PROVISIONS OF FSMA

FSMA prohibits a financial institution from disclosing "nonpublic personal information" to a "nonaffiliated third party" unless the consumer has been provided with an opt-out notice. This disclosure notice must (1) be "clear and conspicuous," (2) be in writing or electronic form, (3) come with an explanation of how to exercise the opt-out or nondisclosure provision, and (4) be given to the consumer before the information is disclosed to a third party. The notice must include any disclosure required under the Fair Credit Reporting Act. *Nonpublic personal information* is defined in the act as "personally identifiable financial information provided by a consumer to a financial institution," resulting from any transaction with or service performed for the consumer. A *nonaffiliated third party* is "any entity that is not an affiliate of, or related by common ownership or affiliated by corporate control with the financial institution." An *affiliate* is "any company that controls, is controlled by, or is under common control with another company."

A disclosure notice is not required for information provided to a supplier of products or services to the financial institution to carry out its business. Services could include direct marketers. However, the two parties must have a contract that requires the supplier to maintain the confidentiality of the consumer's personal information.

When a financial service company establishes a "customer relationship with a consumer, and not less than every 12 months," the company must provide a privacy policy and practices statement describing (1) to whom, how, and what customer information is disclosed to affiliates and nonaffiliates; (2) disclosures of former customer information; and (3) how customer information is protected. Financial institutions cannot disclose a consumer's account number, access number or code, or deposit or transaction account to direct marketers. An exception is made for consumer reporting agencies.

The legislation does not modify or supersede to any extent the Fair Credit Reporting Act (FCRA) of 1970 (15 U.S.C. 1681 et seq.). FCRA regulates methods of obtaining credit information about an applicant or an employee. Essentially, the law requires that an applicant be informed in writing that a credit report is being sought, and the information sought must be defined.

Under FCRA, a credit bureau may provide an employer with a report for "employment purposes," defined as a report used for the purpose of evaluation only. Section 615 of FCRA requires that if the report user denies employment to an individual based wholly or partly on information in the report, he or she must advise the individual and give him or her the name of the credit agency that made the report. Information that causes adverse action must, upon written request from the consumer, be disclosed to the consumer within 60 days. Credit bureaus must delete disputed information if it cannot be verified.

FCRA covers banks, retailers, and other businesses that supply credit bureaus with consumer information. These businesses must take steps to ensure the accuracy of the information collected and investigate disputed information. They can avoid liability if they can show "by a preponderance of the evidence that at the time of the alleged violation [they] maintained reasonable procedures to assure compliance" with the act's accuracy and privacy safeguards.

REQUIRED STUDY OF SHARING OF CONFIDENTIAL INFORMATION BY FINANCIAL INSTITUTIONS

Under FSMA, the Treasury and other federal regulators are charged with conducting a study on the sharing of confidential customer information by financial services companies and their affiliates and nonaffiliated third parties.

The study, mandated for completion by January 1, 2002, will look at

- the level of security,

- risks in sharing confidential information,

- how the information sharing benefits companies and customers,

- the adequacy of existing privacy laws,

- the adequacy of a financial institution's privacy policy,

- the feasibility of notices and opt-in or opt-out alternatives for directing that confidential customer information not be shared, and

- restrictions on information-sharing uses and customer-directed uses of information.

LEGAL PENALTIES UNDER FSMA

Section 521 of FSMA makes it a crime for anyone to obtain or attempt to gain access to customer information from a financial institution through a false, fictitious, or fraudulent statement, document, or representation to an employee or officer of the financial institution. Penalties include fines and imprisonment for up to five years, or both. There are greater penalties for those who engage in a pattern of illegal activity or who violate another U.S. law along with Section 521. Willful misuse of a consumer's personal nonpublic information can trigger punitive damages. FSMA violations also put companies at risk for government enforcement actions and potential class action suits.

CHECKLIST FOR INITIATING FSMA COMPLIANCE

The following items should be used to audit your current privacy policy and practices:

❑ Does your company currently collect personal consumer information?

❑ How is it being collected and processed?

❑ Is it being shared?

❑ How is it being used?

❑ Is it being disclosed to third parties?

❑ Is it being sold, and do you have contractual agreements with the purchasers?

CHECKLIST FOR INITIATING FSMA COMPLIANCE

❏ Who authorizes the collection of information?

❏ For what purpose is the information collected?

❏ Who has access to a customer's private information?

❏ Review contracts with third-party suppliers, especially those providing computer services and data collection.

❏ Review current employee employment policies and confidentiality agreements.

❏ Who oversees privacy policies? Do you have a legal or compliance officer?

❏ What changes in operations will you be required to make under FSMA?

❏ What privacy awareness training will you need, and which departments will be most affected?

❏ Evaluate your website design to make sure it includes clear and conspicuous privacy statements.

❏ What security measures do you need to implement to protect consumer information?

5

INTERNET PRIVACY FOR CHILDREN

Protecting the privacy of children using the Internet has also become a major concern. The Children's Online Privacy Protection Act of 1998 (COPPA) (15 U.S.C. 6501 et seq.) makes it unlawful for website or online service operators to use deceptive practices to collect personal information from a child under the age of 13. COPPA violations are treated as unfair or deceptive trade practices under the Federal Trade Commission Act. A violation of COPPA could result in civil penalties of $11,000 per violation. Persons, partnerships, and corporations are all covered under the act. Regulations to implement COPPA were published by the Federal Trade Commission (FTC) in the *Federal Register* on November 3, 1999 and became effective April 21, 2000.

Under COPPA, a website or online service operator must get a parent's verifiable consent before collecting, using, or disclosing a child's personal information. This consent is similar to an opt-in provision, which requires the operator to seek and obtain positive, affirmative approval and consent to collect and use personal information. Verifiable consent methods are acceptable if they ensure that the person providing the consent is the child's parent or legal guardian.

These methods include sending a confirmatory e-mail to the parent or guardian following receipt of consent or contacting the parent or guardian by telephone or letter to confirm the consent.

COPPA's objective is to protect the privacy of children who use the Internet. The regulations spell out the primary role of parents in controlling how personal information about their children is collected, used, stored, or given to third parties. Collecting personal information from a child includes requesting information online and enabling a child to use a chat room, message board, or e-mail. It also includes passive tracking of an identity code (a "cookie") from a computer. Information that is considered personal includes name, home address, parent's name, phone number, a photograph, an e-mail address, a computer processor serial number, or a cookie.

A website or online service must post a privacy notice detailing the type of information that will be collected, used, secured, and given to third parties. The notice must appear on the website home page and be linked to each area where personal information is collected from children. The notice and links must be placed in a clear and prominent place and not be set in small, "mouse" type. If an operator wants to disclose information to third parties, the site must state the type of business, the purpose of the information use, and whether security and confidentiality of the information are adequate.

Some sites are considered to be "directed to children." The FTC determines whether a site is directed to children by considering such things as its subject matter and content, whether its advertising is obviously aimed at children, its use of animated characters, the presence of child-oriented activities, evidence that the intended audience is children, and whether the child is requested to reveal his or her age while registering at the site.

COPPA REQUIREMENTS

Online operators must

1. provide notice on the website or service of what personal, individually identifiable information it collects from children, and how that information is used or disclosed;

2. obtain verifiable parental consent before collecting, using, or disclosing any information from children;

3. provide a reasonable means for a parent to review any information collected from a child;

4. not require a child to reveal more personal information to participate in a game;

5. establish adequate procedures to protect the confidentiality, integrity, and security of children's personal information;

6. make it possible for parents to review, amend, or delete information collected about their children; refuse to permit further contact with a child; and require the deletion of any information collected; and

7. post a privacy notice on a website home page and provide clear and obvious links to the policy and each area where information is collected from children.

At each step of the information collection process and up to its deletion, the burden is on the operator to inform parents of their rights and the procedures to follow if they wish to change or end the relationship.

COPPA COMPLIANCE AND LIABILITY AUDIT CHECKLIST

The following checklist will help in determining whether an online operator is in compliance with COPPA requirements.

❑ Are you an operator of a commercial website or an online service? Y _____ N _____

❑ Are your services or products entirely or partly directed to children under the age of 13? Y _____ N _____

❑ Do you have actual knowledge that your site is collecting personal information from children under the age of 13? Y _____ N _____

❑ Does your website use automatic and persistent identifiers (computer processor serial numbers, Internet protocol addresses, etc.) or a "cookie" program that tracks visitor information? Y _____ N _____

❏ Do you provide proper notice to parents that your site collects information on children under 13 years old? Y _____ N _____

❏ Before obtaining personal information from children, you are required to obtain explicit, verifiable parental consent to do so; do you use verifiable consent methods to ensure that the person providing the consent is the child's parent or legal guardian? Y _____ N _____

❏ Do you have a posted privacy policy describing the collection method, type of information collected, how it is used, and the disclosure of children's personal information to third parties? Y _____ N _____

❏ Does your policy notice give parents the name and contact information of all operators of the site? Y _____ N _____

❏ Is there an easily accessible and clear link to your privacy policy on your site's home page and in each area where information on children is collected? Y _____ N _____

❏ Are notice links through an icon or text message in plain English, legible, and prominently displayed? Y _____ N _____

❏ Is it your policy and practice that a child should only be required to disclose enough information to participate in a game or contest? Y _____ N _____

❏ Does your site provide parents with an opportunity to review any personal information collected from their children? Y _____ N _____

❏ Would you abide by parents' demands that any information collected by your website about their children be deleted? Y _____ N _____

❏ Would you abide by parents' demands that no personal information be collected from their children in the future? Y _____ N _____

❑ Have you established measures that ensure the confidentiality, integrity, and security of personal information collected from children? Y _____ N _____

❑ Does your privacy policy state that in any disclosures to third parties you have included a description of the third parties, including type of business, how the child's personal information will be used, that third parties must agree to abide by your privacy policy, and that your information security and confidentiality measures are adequate? Y _____ N _____

❑ Have you set up a monitoring program for your website privacy policy and program? Y _____ N _____

❑ Have you set up periodic audits of your privacy program? Y _____ N _____

6

EUROPEAN UNION PRIVACY PROTECTION MANDATE

Privacy protection measures are also in place in Europe. The European Union Directive on Privacy Protection, effective October 1998, required the 15 member countries of the European Union (EU) to adopt tough laws on privacy and to restrict how companies use and transmit personal information outside the EU. *Personal information* includes all data about an individual. The EU Directive restricts the forms of personal information sharing between EU member countries and countries that fail to meet the EU standard for privacy protection.

GENERAL REQUIREMENTS

Under the EU Privacy Directive, personal consumer information may be collected or distributed only

- if it is used for clearly stated and legitimate purposes;

- if the individual consumer gave express consent; and

- if the information is transferred to countries that have adequate privacy protections.

Additional restrictions apply to "sensitive personal data," which includes information about a person's health, race, religious or philosophical beliefs, sexual preferences, ethnic origin, and political or union affiliations.

Members must ensure compliance with the directive by setting up a data "controller" an entity that determines the purposes for and manner in which personal information is collected, processed, and used. In general, individuals have access to all personal information collected by the entity about them and can demand that their personal information be corrected or deleted.

SAFE HARBOR PROGRAMS

The European Union originally determined that the United States did not qualify as a country with adequate personal privacy protections or laws. The directive applies to U.S. companies doing business in EU countries and to companies based in Europe that transfer information to the United States or non-EU countries.

In March 2000, the EU and the United States completed an agreement on how U.S. companies could gather and use personal information from Europeans. Under this "safe harbor" program, a company must agree to

- notify individuals about the types of personal information it wants to collect;

- describe how the personal information will be collected and processed;

- obtain the express consent of an individual before using any information;

- allow individuals to choose what and how personal information will be used by other organizations;

- allow individuals to correct or delete any personal information; and

- allow individuals to deny use of any personal data.

Adequate data security measures that fit the level of information sensitivity must be in place. Companies wanting to comply with the European Union's safe harbor principles should first assess their current data collection practices. This survey should cover the type and extent of information on EU subjects that is collected, processed, stored, and disclosed to third parties, as well as the extent and depth of security and privacy measures. (See the privacy policy checklist in Chapter 5 for an example of questions to be covered by the survey.)

7

INFORMATION PRIVACY AND COMPLIANCE PROGRAMS

As discussed throughout this book, new legislation contains federal criminal sanctions for violations of information security and privacy. The *Federal Sentencing Guidelines* apply to violations of all federal criminal laws. Compliance programs are a means to both mitigate the effects of federal sentencing and provide a framework for e-businesses to establish organization-wide internal controls, policies, safeguards, ethics training, programs, monitoring, and audits to detect and prevent corporate crime.

A business or organization must communicate to its customers, employees, shareholders, suppliers, the government, and the media that it is honest, ethical, and trustworthy, that it complies with laws and regulations. Should things go wrong, if the business is suspected of or charged with a violation of law, one of its first and most valuable defenses is to show that it had an effective compliance program in place prior to the offense.

State and federal governments are requiring compliance programs under a host of statutes. This chapter describes the basic elements common to compliance programs and how organizations can establish effective programs.

"CORPORATE CULTURE" MAY BE A CORPORATE LIABILITY

Every corporation has a "culture" that may be shaped and directed by top management. This "tone at the top" may establish a business climate that tends toward the unethical. An effective compliance program relies on top management to exert direction and resources toward ensuring a corporate culture that is ethical.

In June 2000, the U.S. Department of Justice (DOJ) issued guidelines for federal prosecutors on whether to indict a corporation. These guidelines reflect the belief that management is ultimately responsible for behavior that falls under the *Federal Sentencing Guidelines for Corporations* (FSGO) and the elements of an effective compliance program. The DOJ guidelines cover the following nine factors related to corporate culture:

1. The nature and seriousness of the offense.

2. The pervasiveness of wrongdoing within the organization.

3. An organization's history of similar conduct.

4. Timely and voluntary disclosure of wrongdoing by the organization.

5. Willingness of the organization to cooperate in an investigation.

6. The effectiveness of the organization's compliance program.

7. The organization's remedial actions and restitutional measures.

8. The collateral consequences of a corporate indictment.

9. The adequacy of noncriminal remedies.

The Justice Department's guidelines closely track the due diligence requirements of and use the same vocabulary as the *Federal Sentencing Guidelines for Organizations.*

BENEFITS OF HAVING A COMPLIANCE PROGRAM

The existence of a compliance program is critical for an organization facing a possible indictment. Proof of an effective compliance program may affect a prosecutor's decision to file a criminal or civil charge. Having a compliance program can also be important at the sentencing or damage awards phase because it may militate against a harsh sentence or exorbitant damages.

Other legal and financial benefits of having a compliance program include the following:

- **Lessening of directors' and officers' liability.** In Caremark (*In re Caremark International, Inc. Derivative Litigation* [1996 WL 549894, Delaware Chancery, September 25, 1996]), the Delaware Chancery Court ruled that effective compliance programs could shield directors from liability for the wrongful acts of company managers and employees.

- **Controlling legal costs.** Developing a compliance program requires that an organization be aware of the possible legal risks associated with its business. In essence, this awareness is a form of preventive law that can reduce litigation costs.

- **Maintaining and enhancing corporate reputation.** For many companies, especially those involved in consumer products, financial services, or healthcare, reputation is their most valuable asset. Consumers often make purchasing decisions solely on the reputation of the company and its products or service. A solid compliance program can support a company's good reputation.

- **Succeeding in a global economy.** Businesses often face cultural and economic challenges. A compliance program is the ideal vehicle for preparing employees to deal with acceptable conduct in business contracts and payments, hiring and managing workers, and foreign laws and regulations. Being prepared means avoiding litigation risks that turn into shareholder suits, government prosecution, and bad publicity.

OTHER COMPLIANCE PROGRAM STANDARDS

The DOJ guidelines are part of what is now a comprehensive set of mandates requiring that organizations have effective compliance programs. Under virtually every federal and state criminal statute are requirements "to promulgate and communicate" standards. Following is a list of several key mandating institutions and their requirements.

- The United States Sentencing Commission guidelines for organizations call for ethics policies, codes of conduct, and how to report misconduct; in addition, an organization must have comprehensive and auditable internal controls.

- The Securities and Exchange Commission requires stock brokerages to have supervision policies that are communicated to brokers along with examples of prohibited conduct.

- The Private Securities Litigation Reform Act of 1995 (Public Law 104–67) calls for auditors to examine a publicly traded company's internal controls and assess the effectiveness of compliance programs.

- The American Law Institute's *Principles of Corporate Governance* spell out director liability for inattention to corporate compliance systems.

FEDERAL SENTENCING GUIDELINES: A BIG STICK AND A CARROT

The FSGO are a "big stick," imposing heavy fines and penalties for infractions, "so that the sanctions imposed upon organizations and their agents, taken together, will provide just punishment, adequate deterrence, and incentives for organizations to maintain internal mechanisms for preventing, detecting, and reporting criminal conduct." The guidelines are premised on "black letter" law for liability that "organizations can act only through agents and, under federal criminal law, generally are vicariously liable for offenses committed by their agents. Federal prosecutions of organizations therefore frequently involve individual and organizational co-defendants."

The sentencing guidelines give courts direction on how to structure fines and sentences for corporations and their personnel. The U.S. Sentencing Commission has stated that it intends to allow "the most serious criminal conduct committed by organizations to be punished at or near the statutory maximum levels established by Congress . . . and accommodate the highest fines historically imposed on organizations." In addition, "the court should require the organization to take all appropriate steps to provide compensation to victims and otherwise remedy the harm caused or threatened by the offense."

Activities most likely to result in misconduct should be closely addressed. A liability exposure inventory is a tool to expose these activities.

The basic legal duties of corporate directors are loyalty and care: avoiding conflicts of interest, being informed about company operations, and not making poorly considered decisions or being negligent.

Duty of Care and Negligence

The *duty of care* requirement involves

- foreseeability of harm to the plaintiff;

- the closeness of the connection between the defendant's conduct and the injury incurred;

- the degree of the injury received;

- moral blame attached to the defendant's conduct; and

- existence of a policy of preventing future harm.

Negligence is defined by four elements (W. Keeton, *Prosser and Keeton on Torts,* 1984):

1. A legally recognized duty to act as a reasonable person under the circumstances.

2. A breach of the duty by failing to live up to the standard.

3. A reasonably close causal connection, known as *proximate cause*, which includes cause in fact.

4. Actual loss or damages.

Standards of Liability

Determining whether a company is liable for negligence or failing to exercise the duty of care has been a matter for both courts and legislatures. Various definitions of liability and related concepts have emerged:

- **Strict liability** applies to the act only and requires no proof of intent to commit the act.

- **Vicarious liability.** In general, corporations are vicariously liable for the actionable conduct of their employees performed in the scope of their employment. This traditional doctrine applies to aiding and abetting a crime or a conspiracy to commit a crime or when a person acts with the knowledge and intention of facilitating the commission of a crime.

- **Derivative liability** applies when the actions and intent of corporate officers and agents are imputable to the corporate entity.

- **The responsible corporate officer doctrine** applies to any corporate officer or employee "standing in responsible relation" to a forbidden act. Liability can arise if the officer could have prevented or corrected a violation and failed to do so. This is a critical doctrine with significant implications. An officer has a positive duty to seek out and remedy violations when they occur and a duty to implement measures that will ensure that violations will not occur. The responsible corporate officer doctrine derives from the Food, Drug and Cosmetic Act of 1938 (see *U.S. v. Park*) and the Clean Water Act of 1972. Although normally applied to services and products that affect the health and well-being of the public, the doctrine might be stretched to cover mental well-being, such as privacy. The doctrine forces corporate officers to define which risks they should know because they are likely to be held to an affirmative duty of care concerning those risks.

- **Willful blindness or indifference.** When a company's officers intentionally avoid finding out about a situation or act that will incriminate them, they exhibit *willful* disregard for the governing statute and *indifference* to its requirements.

- **Flagrant organizational indifference** is the conscious avoidance by an organization of learning about and observing the requirements of a statute.

The relationship of corporate directors and officers to stockholders is similar to that of an agent to a principal. Their liability is similar in that it may be based on failure to perform a statutory or common law duty. Failure to use ordinary care and prudence, when it results in loss, can generate liability. An effective compliance program should protect the organization from liability by isolating any rogue employees: those who, for their own benefit, commit illegal acts or whose conduct violates company policy and procedure despite efforts to prevent such acts.

Due Diligence Requirements for an Effective Compliance Program: A Carrot

The *FSGO* have provided a broad legal definition and a blueprint for the establishment of "an effective program to prevent and detect violations of law." An organization that has an effective compliance program has exercised *due diligence*. However, the organization must take a number of concrete and workable actions to *demonstrate* due diligence. The "carrot" of due diligence can mean a reduction in fines (the stick) for organizations convicted of a violation of law.

The compliance program must have been in place and operating before an offense was committed. Further, the program must be tailored to the company's unique corporate culture; correlate with the size, structure, and complexity of the company; and be comparable to other programs in the same industry.

At a minimum, the following steps should be taken to establish an effective compliance program:

1. Establish "compliance standards and procedures . . . reasonably capable of reducing the prospect of criminal conduct." This means written ethics policies and codes of conduct that discourage and deter unethical and illegal behavior. The codes should contain specific prohibitions and be distributed to management and employees.

2. Set up oversight of the compliance program by a "specific individual within high-level personnel of the organization," such as a senior manager, legal counsel, or a compliance officer. This person must be someone of high ethical stature.

3. Use "due care not to delegate substantial discretionary authority" to anyone your organization knew or should have known "had a propensity to engage in illegal activities."

4. Effectively communicate organizational ethics policies and codes of conduct to all employees and agents. This may be done by "requiring participation in training programs or by disseminating publications that explain in a practical manner what is required."

5. Take reasonable steps via monitoring and auditing systems to detect criminal conduct by employees and agents. The *FSGO* imply that an organization needs a full range of safeguards and information systems controls that would detect and deter waste, fraud, and abuse of assets, as well as informal mechanisms related to organizational structure and management controls. In decentralized companies, branches and subsidiaries would need similar controls and audits.

   Audits should review and update codes of conduct, policies, reporting and monitoring procedures, and internal controls. Periodic audits should cover all risk areas, with a focus on the highest compliance risks. Monitoring, like quality checks, should be a routine business practice.

6. Create and publicize a system for reporting criminal conduct in the organization that allows employees to do so without fear of retribution. One way to handle this requirement is for corporate management to issue a policy directive that clarifies when to report criminal conduct, under what circumstances, and to whom. Another is to establish a reporting hotline.

7. Establish disciplinary mechanisms for violations of law as well as for the failure to detect an offense. The "form of discipline that will be appropriate will be case specific." This implies that everyone will be aware of just what *is* a violation of law, and that it is always possible to assess individual liability in a complex organizational structure. This is often not the case.

   Adequate discipline can conflict with union rules and employment laws. Personnel policy manuals may have to state that illegal or unethical conduct is grounds for termination. Managers should always consult with legal counsel before terminating an employee.

8. Take "all reasonable steps to respond appropriately to the offense" once an offense has been discovered, even if not fully verified. An organization must start an internal investigation of the incident. It will be "allowed a reasonable period of time" to conduct it. An incident need not be reported to the "appropriate governmental authorities" if the organization "reasonably concluded, based on the information then available, that no offense had been committed."

   An internal investigation is part of a corporation's defense against possible compliance-related liability. The purpose of the investigation is to gather information for legal advice. Specific actions taken and techniques used in an investigation should be directed at uncovering all information required to clarify the corporation's litigation risk exposure and minimize the damage that could arise from such exposure.

SO YOU HAVE AN EFFECTIVE
COMPLIANCE PROGRAM: PROVE IT!

The implication of the mandates discussed in this chapter is that an organization will have to prove that communication, education, and specific practices comply with statutes and guidelines. A realistic way to approach the need for proof is to look at it as responding to a subpeona or a request for all documents relevant to your compliance program. Of course, legal counsel will be rightly concerned about preserving attorney-client privileges and disclosures. However, a wide range of materials may be required to show that your compliance program is more than a set of manuals sitting on a shelf.

For a start, the internal documents, minutes, or other communications from the board of directors' audit or governance committee to the CEO or compliance officer may reveal the importance placed on establishing the compliance program. Operational evidence could include policies, training materials, job applications, monitoring and auditing reports, and disciplinary actions. Also important are the changes made in policies, codes of conduct, and training/education evaluations. These demonstrate that the program is not static, but ongoing and, hopefully, effective.

SUMMARY

An effective compliance program must be driven from the top down. It must be motivated by top management's understanding of the dangers of prosecution and conviction for illegal acts. Management must be aware that a compliance program can offer possible benefits, including limits on corporate liability and awards for punitive damages, reduction of criminal penalties, and the positive public relations of being viewed as a good corporate citizen. The FSGO offer organizations flexibility in setting up a compliance program. Organizations can identify the acts they must prevent and focus their educational activities on those areas. The compliance program must be active and ongoing, not static. Policies, codes, controls, audits, investigations, enforcement, and responses must be monitored, reviewed, and updated in light of new legal developments and organizational experiences.

8

INTERNAL
PROTECTION
CONTROLS

Management is responsible for establishing effective internal controls that ensure the privacy, security, and integrity of proprietary information and computing/communications systems. The function of an auditor is to examine and attest to the accuracy of the business, financial, and proprietary information and internal controls that safeguard assets from loss. There are internal controls that apply to all companies and that cover all financial, physical, and intellectual assets.

MANAGEMENT CONTROLS: DEFINING INTERNAL CONTROLS AND SAFEGUARDS

A three-year study to develop integrated guidance on internal control was conducted by the Committee of Sponsoring Organizations (COSO), which included the American Institute of Certified Public Accountants (AICPA), the Institute of Internal Auditors (IIA), the Financial Executives Institute (FEI), the Institute of Management Accountants (IMA), and the American Accounting Association (AAA). Their report, *Internal Control—Integrated Framework,* was issued in 1992.

The report is designed to provide a common definition of *internal control* and establish a standard by which companies can assess their system of internal controls. As described in the report, every system of internal control has its limitations. However, it is COSO's view that if management, boards of directors, external auditors, and others adopt the components, criteria, and guidelines set forth in the report, incidents of fraudulent financial reporting and other control breaches will be reduced.

The report tries to establish a definition of internal control in the hope that laws and regulations will adopt an agreed-upon nomenclature. The study defines *internal control* as a process, "effected by an entity's board of directors, management and other personnel, designed to provide reasonable assurance regarding the achievement of objectives in . . . effectiveness and efficiency of operations, reliability of financial reporting, [and] compliance with applicable laws and regulations." The study points out that five interrelated components of internal control must be present and functioning to have an effective control system:

1. **Control environment.** The integrity, ethical values, and competence of the entity's people; management's philosophy and operating style; the way management assigns authority and responsibility and organizes and develops its people; and the attention and direction provided by the board of directors.

2. **Risk assessment.** The identification and analysis of relevant risks to achievement of objectives, forming a basis for determining how risks should be managed.

3. **Control activities.** The policies and procedures that help ensure management directives are carried out, including activities as diverse as approvals, authorizations, verifications, reconciliations, reviews of operating performance, security of assets, and segregation of duties.

4. **Information and communication.** Information about external events plus clear messages from top management that control responsibilities must be taken seriously.

5. **Monitoring.** A process that assesses the quality of the system's performance over time.

After several months of discussion, in May 1994, COSO published an addendum to the report providing more detail on safeguarding controls. Shortly thereafter, then-U.S. Comptroller General Bowsher wrote COSO, stating that "the addendum provides a good working definition of safeguarding controls and criteria for judging their effectiveness. We support the COSO position that it is important for management reports to external parties on controls over financial reporting to also cover controls over safeguarding of assets. . . . With the addendum, we believe the COSO Framework merits general acceptance for evaluating the effectiveness of internal controls." Bowsher indicated that the COSO standards would be considered in the next revision of the Government Accounting Office's *Yellow Book* of rules for government accounting.

The COSO addendum defines a new internal control category: "internal control over safeguarding of assets against unauthorized acquisition, use or disposition is a process, effected by an entity's board of directors, management and other personnel, designed to provide reasonable assurance regarding prevention or timely detection of unauthorized acquisition, use or disposition of the entity's assets that could have a material effect on the financial statements." This new category is "a subset of the broader segment of internal control described as safeguarding of asset controls." *Authorization,* in the addendum, includes "approval of transactions in accordance with policies and procedures established by management and the board of directors to safeguard assets."

ACCOUNTING PROFESSION COMPLIANCE AUDITS STANDARD

The purpose of a compliance audit is to assist users—regulators, the board of directors, and contract officers—in evaluating management's assertions. The users also decide the procedures to be performed in the audit; these are called *agreed-upon procedures.* To evaluate the effectiveness of an entity's internal control structure for compliance, its management can use the COSO criteria and general framework. However, for some compliance areas more detailed and specialized criteria may be needed, for example from a regulatory agency.

The American Institute of Certified Public Accountants auditing standards board has issued Statement on Standards for Attestation Engagements (SSAE) no. 3, *Compliance Attestation.* This standard applies to independent accountants hired by the management of an entity to evaluate management's written assertion about the entity's compliance with laws, regulations, rules, or grants; assess the effectiveness of the entity's internal control structure over compliance; or both of the above. These audits are requested by an organization, but they can help satisfy a regulatory agency and others that the organization is in compliance. Outside auditors may be called on to review the current compliance efforts and suggest ways in which the organization can beef up its internal controls over compliance.

SSAE no. 3 emphasizes management's responsibility for

a) identifying applicable compliance requirements

b) establishing and maintaining internal control structure policies and procedures to provide reasonable assurance that the entity complies with those requirements

c) evaluating and monitoring the entity's compliance

d) specifying reports that satisfy legal, regulatory, or contractual requirements.

PRINCIPLES OF COMPUTER CONTROLS

A "control" is any device, action, or procedure that reduces the risk of asset loss. In a computer, for example, there may be access control software or a biometric device that authenticates and verifies the identity of a user seeking to access the computer system. For example, in an accounting/purchasing system, a control may be validity checks that are designed to

- separate duties between those with property *handling* responsibilities and those with property *recording* responsibilities;

- determine that (1) a purchase has been approved by someone with authority to commit funds for such purposes, (2) a purchase is from a vendor who is approved, (3) a purchase is by a person who is authorized to buy, (4) specific goods ordered were in fact received, and (5) the unit price charged and extensions are stated correctly on the vendor's invoice; and

- provide an oversight mechanism at each step in processing a transaction to detect errors, omissions, and improprieties in the previous step. This can be accomplished through division of labor and dual responsibility for related transactions (e.g., counter signature, segregation of functions, dollar authorization limits). The oversight mechanism should prevent fraudulent transactions by making it necessary for at least two parties to be in collusion for such acts to occur.

Validity checks involve authorization procedures established to determine whether a payment is based on a legitimate claim against the company by a vendor or supplier who has in fact supplied something of corresponding value.

SECURITY VULNERABILITIES AND CONTROL ISSUES

Electronic Commerce

There are a number of vulnerabilities in electronic commerce:

- Lack of authentication of transaction authorization.

- Interception of data by outsiders.

- Lack of physical access control to the computer system.

- An inadequate and weak access control system.

- The introduction of computer viruses into networked systems.

- Inadequate control over storage media.

- A single user in a microcomputer system authorizing and recording transactions.

- Management software that specifies limits to dollar amounts of signatures.

- Low or absent management awareness and support of computer security measures.

- Users having the ability to enter a range of specific data-base choices.

- Sensitive fields being available on data entry screens.

- Users downloading accounting information to personal computers.

- Critical computer file backup procedures not being enforced.

- Multilevel password control systems not being used.

- Password-controlled disk lock system not being used.

- Networks not being protected by any type of firewall, such as screening routers or an operating system or application-based system.

- Cryptography not being used in either computer communications or storage systems.

Employee Screening Policies and Background Investigation

To prevent security vulnerabilities, companies should conduct the following background inquiries about employee applicants:

- **Criminal records.** Use public records to obtain criminal histories. (See additional discussion, below.)

- **Driving records.** If an applicant may be driving a company car, obtain a driving record from the state motor vehicle department. (See additional discussion, below.)

- **Past employment references.** Employers should attempt to contact past employers and document information. The applicant should be asked for names of four or five people he or she reported to at each of the last four or five positions. (See additional discussion, below.)

- **Education and credential verification.** Contact educational institutions named by the applicant or state licensing boards. (See additional discussion, below.)

- **Credit standing.** It may be necessary to use an outside agency to stay in compliance with the Fair Credit Reporting Act.

- **Preemployment assessments.** Personality assessments can provide an indication of the characteristics a person displays over time, such as trustwothiness or emotional stability. Attitudinal assessments provide an indication of a person's attitudes about work-related issues, such as honesty.

- **Preemployment structured interviews.** These interviews are designed to go into more depth, based on information from sources listed above, to further develop the applicant's profile.

Hiring a bad employee can be disastrous. Further complicating the hiring process is the growing use of the legal doctrine of negligent hiring, which imposes a duty on employers to assess the nature of the job and its degree of risk to third parties, then perform a reasonable background investigation to ensure that the applicant is competent and fit for employment. If an employee hired for a position in which there is a considerable degree of risk to third parties later causes harm, the employer may have to defend its hiring decision.

Employers will often opt to use a screening service simply because they are unable to obtain contact information for sources of public record and background information. The *Guide to Background Investigations* (Total Information Services, 8th ed., 1998) includes contact information on public record sources. Using the following record sources during a background check should provide evidence that a good faith screening effort was made during the hiring process:

1. **Criminal records.** A criminal records search should be the cornerstone of a company's preemployment procedures. Obtaining criminal histories on each and every potential employee will reduce exposure to negligent hiring litigation, employee theft, and workplace violence. Further, in negligent hiring lawsuits, courts and juries generally side with employers who can document a bona fide attempt to investigate the applicant's criminal record.

2. **Driving records.** If the position being filled will involve the employee driving a motor vehicle on public streets, a driving record should be obtained. For nondriving positions, a check may reveal that the applicant has a record of drunk or reckless driving convictions.

3. **Past employment.** Past employers may give valuable information on an applicant's past performance, although derogatory information may be excluded. Document all information, or lack of it. Look for time gaps in an employment history and for references that appear to be unreliable.

4. **Education and credential verification.** In many fields, liability can be directly related to an employee's qualifications for a specific position. Contacting educational institutions and state licensing boards may ensure that an individual hired for a position is qualified to perform the job adequately and without risks to clients or the general public.

Employee Behavior: Overcontrol or Undercontrol?

Establishing effective and efficient management controls tends to be a matter of balancing costs against benefits. Tipping the balance to either extreme of overcontrol or undercontrol is inefficient and ineffective. The cost of implementing controls is far easier to calculate than the intended benefits of such controls because costs tend to be quantitative, whereas benefits tend to be qualitative. Deciding how much control should be exercised in any organization is not a simple matter. Economic and behavioral considerations include direct and consequential costs (acquisition, implementation, and maintenance).

Behavioral considerations have to do with the impact controls may have on employees. To evaluate the behavioral costs of controls, ask the following questions:

- Do controls take on the aura of absolute rules, prohibitions, and mandatory actions and thus discourage use of judgment and discretion?

- What impact do controls have on personal productivity?

- Do control costs affect human performance and job satisfaction?

When controls are designed and enforced without rationality, need, or consideration for the sensitivities of the people affected by them, slavish compliance is required. Slavish and irrational controls make people angry, and they take revenge by seeing if they can circumvent or violate those controls. Covert and overt resistance can follow. In fact, in some organizational settings, overcontrol often results in petty acts of fraud and thievery (e.g., lying on expense accounts and "fudging" performance data).

Responses to Controls

Accountants, auditors, and security people are the most control-minded employees in any organization, as indeed they should be to properly discharge their missions. But they often erroneously assume that employees who will have to live with controls will accept them out of pure logic, rationality, and good business judgment. To their dismay, those in charge of implementing controls feel abused and frustrated when their designs are not welcomed with open arms. Pockets of resistance develop even before they attempt to implement their grand new ideas. But why? Don't the employees understand their good and honorable intentions?

Employees do understand that those in charge of implementing controls are only trying to do their jobs. But that does not cause them to feel sympathy for the implementers and the proposed changes. Any change tends to cause resistance. The reason for resistance is that change may be perceived by the employees as a threat to their economic security; their power base, authority, status, job role, or job relationships; or the status quo. Responses to change take a variety of forms, depending on the employee's level of authority.

- **Aggression:** hitting back (e.g., sabotaging the new system or controls)—mainly nonmanagers

- **Projection:** blaming new difficulties on the implementers or their "bright ideas" or devices—mainly middle managers

- **Avoidance:** stubbornly refusing to comply—most common among top management

Overcoming Resistance to Controls

An organization can overcome resistance to or negative reactions to controls by taking the following actions:

1. Make sure that goals, objectives, and control standards are realistic, not impossible or improbable of achievement. Standards, goals, and objectives should be challenging but attainable with ordinary, not extraordinary, effort.

2. Involve the employees who will be bound by the standards in the control-setting process.

3. Install controls only where they are necessary for prudent management and evaluate their continued need and enhancement periodically. Remember, the real enemies to good and effective controls are undercontrol and overcontrol.

4. Place administration and monitoring of tight controls as far down in the organization as possible. Otherwise, the "brass" gets too bogged down in detail and "control trivia," and lower-level managers become more and more like police officers.

5. Give output controls a slight edge over behavioral controls. Monitor the quantity and quality of output against the present standard. Behavioral controls, like personal observations, are best used when performance requirements are clear and generally known. Surveillance here is perceived as less obtrusive. In fact, if coupled with positive reinforcements, such surveillance can promote efficiency and motivation. Both output and behavioral controls play important roles in achieving organizational objectives.

6. Don't expect new and better controls in and of themselves to solve problems. Together with enlightened management, good administration, and intelligent interpretation, controls lead to efficient and effective operations.

7. Differentiate between the two types of controls: before the fact and after the fact. Before-the-fact controls are intended to prevent problems from occurring. They pinpoint violations of established policies and procedures and spot errors in input accuracy and validity. After-the-fact controls are intended to detect problems that may quickly grow out of control and require immediate remedy.

8. Make sure rules are fair, rational, and needed for orderly procedure. They will be better complied with than if their breach just carries the threat of punishment.

Where controls are admittedly less than adequate, overcome resistance to change by applying the following general rules:

- Change incrementally, a little at a time, not radically.

- Involve the people or a representative grouping of people on whom the major burden of adjustment to change will be required early in the planning or decision-making process.

- Communicate the reasons for the change: cost savings, theft reduction, loss prevention, prudence, regulatory requirement, and so forth.

- Focus on the benefits of the change to the organization itself and its people.

- Relate the new controls to meaningful and accepted corporate goals.

- *Do not* overcontrol. The costs always outweigh the benefits.

- Provide employees with adequate resources, training, and support to get the job done right.

- Promote trusting relationships among all levels of management, between peers and between management and nonmanagement personnel.

COMMON INADEQUACIES IN A CONTROL ENVIRONMENT

Following is a list of the most common problems in an organization's control environment:

1. Inadequate rewards for employee performance.

2. Insufficient internal controls, in particular, a lack of suitable separation of duties or audit trails.

3. Ambiguity in employee job roles, duties, responsibilities, and areas of accountability.

4. Failure to counsel employees and to take suitable administrative action when performance levels or personal behavior falls below acceptable levels.

5. Lack of timely periodic audits, inspections, and operational reviews and a failure of senior executives to follow up on their results to ensure that the organization's goals, priorities, policies, and procedures—as well as relevant government regulations—are being complied with.

6. Insufficient orientation and training of employees and executives about legal, ethical, and security issues and the organization's policies for resolving them.

7. Inadequate organizational policies regarding sanctions for legal, ethical, and security breaches and a failure of senior executives to monitor and enforce these policies.

9

CREATING AND COMMUNICATING POLICIES

Through its policies, a company can assert its right to supervise and ensure an efficient and secure workplace. The objective is to produce policies that provide clear, accurate, and persuasive communication on required conduct for employees. Policies are a means of educating employees about ethical and legal obligations, with the goal of reducing potential litigation risks for the company. Policies also foster a company climate of recognizing an obligation to obey laws and of not tolerating acts that skirt or breach laws. Policies indicate both a goal and a promise to implement practices that will achieve, in this case, the privacy and security of personal information.

Policy creation and education require a collaborative effort. A policy development team should include legal counsel familiar with both computer law and liability exposures the company may face, human resources management, computer systems and security personnel who know the computer and communications equipment and how employees use it, and auditors experienced with compliance audits.

Basic guidelines for policy formation require that policies

- be in written form,

- be current,

- mean what they say,

- be kept in a single repository,

- be in plain English, and

- be comprehensive.

POLICIES FROM THE TOP

Organizations that have a board of directors or outside owners may produce "executive limitations" policies to ensure that the chief executive officer (CEO) or manager carries out duties in a prudent and ethical manner. For example, the board may direct the CEO not to allow corporate assets to be unprotected or unnecessarily placed at risk. Intellectual property and proprietary information assets may be specifically cited along with physical and financial assets. The noteboard may also officially direct the CEO not to endanger the company's public image or take any action that is imprudent or unethical.

ETHICS AND CODES OF CONDUCT

At levels below the CEO, policies may define unethical and imprudent behavior as well as specific assets to be protected. Policies should specifically forewarn employees of the consequences of prohibited acts. Ethics policies and codes of conduct must be written down and should explicitly discourage and deter unethical and illegal behavior. These codes should contain specific prohibitions against: abuse and misuse of computer systems; theft; embezzlement; fraud; destruction of company property; falsifying attendance, payroll, production, and expense reports; gambling on company time and property; and sexual harassment. The company should distribute the codes to management and employees.

Controlling unethical conduct in organizations is largely a matter of role modeling. If executives and supervisors behave ethically, employees tend to conform to an ethical standard. After role modeling, the next best approach is the establishment of a corporate code of ethics and an anticrime policy. Written codes of conduct, adopted and adhered to by top management, can have a positive effect in deterring unlawful behavior in the organization. However, establishing a code doesn't end the company's responsibility. The company must enforce the code, spelling out enforcement procedures so that violations are reported, investigated, and resolved.

When attempting to control and reduce abusive or criminal acts, management must communicate clearly to employees that such acts are considered to be and will be treated as a serious problem. The major impact of a policy is that it conveys to employees the organization's concern and unambiguously communicates that abuse of company property will result in punishment.

DEVELOPING A POLICY

There are three main points to keep in mind when developing a policy:

1. It is a good idea to have the outline of any policy reviewed or even written by legal counsel. The final draft must be reviewed and approved by the responsible company officer and counsel.

2. The policy should be reviewed periodically and updated in light of new legal developments and corporate experiences.

3. The policy is not an employment contract.

When creating a new policy or replacing an existing one, the following six steps should be taken:

1. Analyze the current policy (if any).

2. Find out how employees currently use equipment or systems.

3. Examine current law covering privacy, prohibited conduct, and telecommunications use.

4. Conduct a litigation risk assessment for the affected areas of your company and develop a vulnerability chart of critical legal risks for the company, its agents, and its customers. A litigation risk assessment is an organization-specific examination of potential legal liabilities, such as inadequate or absent security measures for the privacy of personal, nonpublic information. Such a security lapse

could lead to the unwanted disclosure of personal information, resulting in legal problems.

5. Review current protection measures against liability, including controls, security, monitoring, audits, and insurance.

6. Review the status of your compliance program.

Include in any policy a clear statement prohibiting specific illegal actions affecting fixed or liquid company assets. The policy should cover misuse of the company's computing and communications systems, other related systems, and equipment that could be used to perform any unauthorized or prohibited acts.

PROMULGATING THE POLICY

Communicate the policy to employees through an employee handbook (maintain a log of employees who receive the handbook), a posting on employee bulletin boards, or through physical or electronic distribution of the text. Recipients should sign off, initial, and date their copies of the policy.

Effective communication of a policy requires explaining in plain English what behavior is required of employees. The communication must also be specific about wrongdoing to be avoided and directed at those who may be in a position to violate the law. The materials must educate and inform employees about their compliance responsibilities.

Evaluate your policy communication by using fog indexes* or having interviewers test the comprehension and understanding of the policy among employees on a random or statistical basis. Communication and education are at the core of an effective policy or code of conduct. A communica-

---

*Most legal writing is "fog," meaning that it is unnecessarily complex and dense, using few active verbs and too many words. The Fog Index Scale, developed by Robert Gunning in 1944, is a means for measuring the complexity of prose.

tions program must be ongoing, reflecting changes in a company's perceived risks and responding to new legal and regulatory mandates. The program must maintain a strategy of testing and proving that the message is getting through to affected personnel.

REPORTING SYSTEMS

The company should create and publicize a system for reporting possible criminal conduct inside the organization that allows employees to do so without fear of retribution. There are several ways to handle this requirement. A policy directive from corporate management should clarify when to report a possible illegal act, under what circumstances, and to whom. In addition, policy statements should state that suspected wrongdoing will be investigated thoroughly and that suspects will be treated consistently without regard to position in the company or length of service.

INVESTIGATIVE RESPONSES

As soon as an offense has been discovered, even if it has not yet been fully verified, the company must immediately take all reasonable steps to respond appropriately to the offense.

This means that the company must conduct an internal investigation of the incident and complete it within a reasonable period of time. Responsibility for conducting an investigation should be clearly assigned to internal auditing, security, legal counsel, or outside investigators. An incident need not be reported to any appropriate governmental authorities if the company, based on the information then available, concludes that no criminal or compliance-related offense has been committed.

The company should have in place a systematic records and document retention and destruction program to meet legitimate business needs and legal obligations, including internal investigations. If a criminal act is uncovered, the company must report to and cooperate with law enforcement agencies. Investigative results must also be reported to the audit committee. The company may report an incident to its bonding company if required to do so under an insurance policy.

VIOLATIONS AND ENFORCEMENT OF POLICY

Enforcement of policy and sanctions applied to violations of policy must be consistent. A policy should spell out clearly and specifically

- the disciplinary mechanisms for illegal conduct, unethical conduct, and failure to detect an offense;
- conduct that is grounds for termination;
- that disciplinary measures will not conflict with employment or federal labor laws or union rules;
- that disciplinary measures will apply to supervisors, managers, and executives who condone questionable, improper, or illegal conduct by those reporting to them or who fail to take appropriate corrective action when such matters are brought to their attention;
- that termination action will not conflict with the personnel manual (the policy should spell out precisely what the company would do to anyone harming or misusing equipment or stealing company property and that management will consult legal counsel on termination actions); and
- that the legal department will report periodically to management and the audit committee each confirmed violation of the policy of which it has knowledge.

If the company policy on illegal behavior has an immediate termination/no exceptions clause, the company had better be prepared to defend it. Although such a clause may be consistent with overall company policy on violations, most companies prefer a two- or three-stage procedure, moving through warning, to counseling/reminding of the policy, then finally to termination or prosecution. An alternative to the immediate termination clause could state: "Violation of corporate policies by employees will invoke disciplinary measures up to and including termination." Company policy regarding prosecution should always be clearly stated and be issued in the name of the CEO. The prosecution policy should include a requirement that anticipated prosecutive actions be reviewed with legal counsel prior to their initiation.

AUDITS OF POLICY COMPLIANCE

An audit of policy compliance is designed to determine whether the company complies with its own policy directives and procedures. Such audits are conducted by the internal audit department, which should

- set the frequency and timing of audits,

- focus on formal and informal management controls and assess their effectiveness,

- thoroughly review all controls in each area, and

- document and report findings to the audit committee of the board of directors.

WORKPLACE PRIVACY AND LIABILITY ISSUES

An employer is vicariously liable for the illegal acts of employees who are acting "within the scope of their employment." This may include "acts" committed via computing or communications systems. An emerging legal concept is the tort of negligent supervision, or failing to supervise an offending employee. Organizations are faced with both lower standards of liability and mandates to report possible regulatory, civil, or criminal misconduct of employees or the organization itself.

Areas of contention in employee privacy and security include

- Arrest/criminal records

- Bank information (checking account, safe deposit boxes, loans)

- Credit information reporting

- Medical records

- Employment records

- Tax records

- Education records

- Use of investigative agencies/background investigations

- Use of polygraph (at any stage of employment)

- Use of psychological tests

- Use of personal identification/verification methods; "active badge/sensor" location and tracking

- Use of "service or performance monitoring" methods, software, or equipment

- Use of electronic/video surveillance; computer screen snapshots

- Secret or investigative files or dossiers

- Internal control, screening, or detection procedures or equipment

- Employee personnel files, which must contain job-related information only yet comply with various federal wage-hour and EEO recordkeeping requirements as well as records retention policies set by existing federal, state, and local laws or regulations

- Searches of workplace lockers, desks, files, computers, and storage media

- Compilations of an employee's internet usage: e-mail sent, websites visited, and files downloaded

- Telephone call accounting of all employee phone calls at the workplace

- Drug testing: random, periodic, or for probable cause

COMMUNICATIONS SYSTEM POLICY CONSIDERATIONS

The primary employee misuses of communications systems are: excessive personal use of the system; use for an outside business; personal investing, gambling, or accessing pornography; infringing intellectual property rights; and sending malicious and harmful messages.

This section focuses on the privacy and security of elements of a communications system, such as the internet, bulletin boards, and websites. These systems may also transmit information to the public, thus affecting the potential liability exposure of the organization.

To control and limit the misuse of an organization's communications system, there must be a policy and set of procedures that cover

- network and computer hardware and software, and connections to online services and other networks;

- the ownership of the communications system and purposes for which it is to be used;

- fair, nondiscriminatory treatment of all employees;

- electronic messages that are obscene, offensive, or project discrimination, harassment, or any form of abuse;

- enforcement and penalties for misuse; and

- a preventive law awareness program for communications system users.

A company must deal with the expectation of privacy with respect to e-mail and other elements of the communications system. The organization should promulgate a clear statement on communications system privacy designed to eliminate employee expectations of privacy and assert employer ownership, authority, and oversight of the communications system. It should be clear that employee use of the communications system is at the employer's discretion. The employee must abide by rules and restrictions designed to protect the employer's property and serve legitimate business interests, such as the employer's need to identify messages and acts that might compromise the employer's legal interests. Policies, rules, and actions should clarify that

- individual access to the communications system is via security-controlled mechanisms and is administered by security or network administrators,

- the network may be monitored and message content filtered, and

- system-generated files may be searched and seized at any time and for any reason.

The prohibitions on communications system monitoring and disclosure in the Electronic Communications Privacy Act (ECPA) of 1986 exempt business uses, specifically allowing

> an officer, employee, or agent of a provider of wire or electronic communication service, whose facilities are used in the transmission of a wire communication, to intercept, disclose, or use that communication in the normal course of his employment while engaged *in any activity which is a necessary incident to the rendition of his service or to the protection of the rights or property of the provider of that service* [emphasis added].

Another clause of the ECPA allows interception of communications if the "electronic device" used for interception is

> any telephone or telegraph instrument, equipment or facility, or component thereof, furnished to the subscriber or user in the ordinary course of business and being used by the subscriber or user in the ordinary course of its business

or furnished by such subscriber or user for connection to the facilities of such services and *used in the ordinary course of its business* [emphasis added].

Presumably, monitoring and filtering software meet the definition of "component thereof." The ECPA only covers the interception of electronic communications transmitted via common carrier.

COMMUNICATIONS SYSTEM POLICY LANGUAGE

The external and internal corporate electronic communications systems that should be covered are

- microcomputers, terminals, and networks; and
- messages, drafts, records, documents, and other information on the communications system, including backup media and storage.

  Sample content language for the policy follows:

- The sole purpose of the Corporation's communications system is to assist in conducting the business of the enterprise.

- All computers and communications equipment and facilities and the data and information stored on them are to remain at all times business property of the Corporation and are to be used for business purposes only.

- It is the goal of the Corporation to maintain a work environment for all its employees without disparate treatment. The Corporation will not tolerate abuse or discrimination against candidates or existing employees.

- Messages on the Corporation's communications system may not contain language or images that may be reasonably considered offensive, demeaning, or disruptive to any employee or create a discriminatorily hostile or abusive work environment. Forbidden content includes, but is not limited to, sexually explicit comments or images, gender-specific comments, racial epithets and slurs, or any comments or images that would offend someone based on race, color, sex, religion, national origin, age, physical or mental disability, status as a veteran, or sexual orientation.

- The Corporation reserves the right to monitor all communications system message content.

- Any views expressed by individual employees in communications system messages are not necessarily those of the Corporation.

- The Corporation will put in place a systematic communications system message, records, and document retention and destruction program designed to meet the legitimate business needs and legal obligations of the Corporation.

- Violation of Corporate policies by employees will result in disciplinary measures up to and including termination.

- This policy will be reviewed periodically and updated in light of new legal developments and Corporate experiences.

WEBSITE PRIVACY SEALS AND STANDARDS

WebTrust is a privacy seal developed in 1998 by the American Institute of Certified Public Accountants (AICPA). The privacy seal is granted to a company's website if its privacy practices and controls reveal the following:

- The specific kinds of information collected and used and any uses by third parties,

- How private information is collected online and used by the company,

- What happens if a consumer refuses to give private information,

- How private information is revised and corrected,

- How website information tracking devices are used and how the consumer may refuse to accept such a device, and

- The security measures to ensure privacy of consumers' information.

The Open Profiling Standard (OPS) provides a voluntary framework covering the collection and sharing of personal information supplied by consumers visiting sites on the Web while assuring their privacy. The Web user receives a common electronic form for listing personal information, such as marital status, home ownership, hobbies, and other relevant marketing-related information. Users are notified when a website requests personal information. Users can give the site some or all of their personal information. The website must obtain the users' consent to give any personal information to another business or site.

The Platform for Privacy Preferences (P3)1999 is a broader standard than OPS and creates a common set of computer codes that allow a website to transmit its privacy policies to a user's browser software. The user can then use the browser to communicate with websites that meet the user's criteria for privacy. Currently, sites often use "cookies" that can be read from or written to a user's hard drive. Data collection software routines and these cookie files stored on a user's computer can reveal the names of websites recently visited and activities during a visit, such as a transaction. The World-Wide Web Consortium (W3C), which has a 170-company membership, put together the P3 privacy initiative with the same goal as the Open Profiling Standard. W3C members Netscape and Microsoft will have browsers that will support P3.

10

DIGITAL SIGNATURES LIBERATE ELECTRONIC COMMERCE

Both consumer and business-to-business marketing require the same interrelationships between trust, reputation, loyalty, privacy/confidentiality, and security. *Digital trust* refers to secure transactions via the Internet, virtual private networks, or wireless communications. Security technologies of digital signatures, biometrics, encryption, network/computer access, and intrusion controls may be used to provide assurance of authenticity and integrity for electronic transactions or messages. Without secure and private communications, electronic contracts would be unenforceable and e-commerce would not be possible. The technologies that make e-commerce viable are described in this chapter and in Chapters 11 and 12.

In June 2000, the U.S. Congress passed, and President Clinton signed, the Millennium Digital Commerce Act, authorizing the use of electronic signatures in nearly all commercial transactions. Under the act, an *electronic signature* is defined as "an electronic sound, symbol, or process attached to or logically associated with a record and executed or adopted by a person with the intent to sign the record." *Record* means "information that is inscribed on a tangible medium or that is stored in an electronic or other medium and is retrievable in perceivable form."

The aim of Congress in passing the law was to encourage expansion of electronic commerce, provide a consistent legal foundation across multiple jurisdictions, and permit and encourage the use and development of technology-neutral electronic signature technologies. The purposes of the act are to:

1. permit and encourage the continued expansion of electronic commerce through the operation of free market forces rather than proscriptive governmental mandates and regulations;

2. promote public confidence in the validity, integrity, and reliability of electronic commerce and online control under federal law;

3. facilitate and promote electronic commerce by clarifying the legal status of electronic signatures in the context of contract formation;

4. facilitate the ability of private parties engaged in interstate transactions to agree among themselves on the appropriate electronic signature technologies for their transactions; and

5. promote the development of a consistent national legal infrastructure necessary to support electronic commerce at the federal and state levels in existing areas of jurisdiction.

In any transaction affecting interstate commerce, a contract cannot be denied legal enforceability solely because an electronic signature or record was used in its formation. However, the act does not apply to any of the following:

- The Uniform Commercial Code, except sections 1-107 and 1-206, Article 2 and 2A

- Premarital agreements, marriage, adoption, divorce, wills, or other matters of family law

- Title documents that are filed on record with a government unit (until a particular state chooses to accept filings electronically)

- Residential landlord-tenant relationships

- The Uniform Health Care Decisions Act of as in effect in a particular state

- Any state that has adopted the Uniform Electronic Transactions Act of 1990

- Crucial notices, such as utility cutoffs, insurance cancellations, and mortgage foreclosures

This law encourages the federal government to promote electronic transactions by removing paper-based obstacles, allowing parties to prove in court that their authentication methods and transactions are valid, and analyzing specific laws administered by a federal agency that may impose a barrier to electronic transactions or to doing business online. This last provision is forced on agencies by a provision in the act that requires a review of agency regulations that might adversly affect electronic commerce.

HOW TO USE ELECTRONIC SIGNATURES

Consumers now have a choice for legally enforceable contracts for health insurance, banking, and opening brokerage accounts: traditional paper and "wet" signatures or electronic signatures. Parties may choose the electronic/digital signature they want to use. The consumer will receive a test document/e-mail confirming that the computer systems are compatible, that documents can be read and stored. The consumer may consent to receiving electronic documents. Consumers should be told they have the right to receive hard copy documents. An enrollment procedure will be unique for the particular type of digital signature. The validity of the digital signature must be established, that is, to verify that the digital signature can be identified as belonging to a particular person and that the signature represents an affirmative act of that person. For an electronic contract to be invalid, it must be illegal or unconscionable or have some other fatal flaw.

WHAT THE DIGITAL SIGNATURES ACT LEAVES UNDONE

The act does not address the following important issues:

1. Are electronic signatures writings under, for example, the statute of frauds?

2. There is no mandate for setting standards for ensuring the security of biometric devices.

3. How is jurisdiction determined in cyberspace?

4. There are no consumer privacy standards for the use of digital signatures.

5. There are no online security standards.

6. What defines *misuse of a digital signature*? What are the liability and recovery for damages?

7. Should potential conflicts be specified in contracts?

8. What should be done when one party says a contract has been changed after signing?

9. With the risks and threats in cyberspace poorly defined and unclear, how can comprehensive, cost-effective security be devised?

These questions will eventually be answered through additional legislation and court cases. Standards for security devices and systems will also be forthcoming, but it is unclear at this point when they will be developed.

11

BIOMETRIC SECURITY SYSTEMS

In the security context, *biometrics* is the machine/computer identification and verification of users based on biological or physiological measurements. In general operation, the system consists of a device that scans or replicates the characteristic to be measured. The device may record a series of words; photograph or laser scan a fingerprint or an eye's vessel pattern; or measure the length of a person's fingers and the spread of the hand, the speed, pressure and size of a person's signature, or the speed and rhythm of keystrokes in data entry. The computer and appropriate software store, process, and analyze the measurements.

Biometrics has been tested and in use more than 30 years. Military, intelligence, and research facilities have experimented with and run tests on a variety of biometric-based access control security systems. Some early biometrics were based on such unique personal identifiers as ear prints, lip prints, blood vessel patterns, voiceprints, and computer-supported skill tests. Biometric systems have a much wider use today because computing power has increased and costs have gone down. We now have a good selection of devices that can scan, discriminate, and analyze distinct biometric data.

In controlling access to a computer, database, or network, the goal is to have a system based on positive identification of the user, to verify that users are who they claim to be. A positive ID system should provide both security and an accurate and legally convincing audit trail for financial/information transactions, supply-chain management, or investigations of computer-related fraud.

HOW BIOMETRIC SYSTEMS OPERATE

In a biometric system, each user is enrolled by the system and a copy of the enrollment data is stored on a database. This first sample of biometric data from a user may be compressed, encrypted, and stored in a database or on a *smart card* (discussed below). For authentication, a new scan is compared to the one stored in the database.

Software, called application programming interface (API), allows use of biometric technology to communicate with operating. This means that users may simply plug in biometric devices and log on to their computers.

BIOMETRIC IDENTIFICATION/ VERIFICATION TECHNIQUES

The major biometric security techniques in use today are described below.

- **Facial scanning.** Also called *facial thermogram or mapping,* this technique relies on an algorithm for pattern recognition unique to an individual's face. A system may mimic the brain's methods of recognizing faces, analyzing bone curvature or the positioning and size of a face's major features. These systems are increasingly used at ATMs and computer terminals.

  A small video camera is connected to a computer. The person seeking access looks into the camera and the scanning verifies or rejects the person depending on the scanning match. A camera can continuously view terminal users and confirm their identity. If an authorized person leaves or another sits down at the terminal, the security system's facial recognition algorithm can trigger a sign-off by the original terminal user and require a sign-on by the new user.

- **Fingerprints.** A computerized system uses electro-optical recognition and file matching of fingerprint details such as ridges, points and whorls, or the ends of lines or breaks in the lines of a print. Newer systems measure the level of heat left on a scanner from a fingerprint impression or analyze the electrical charges emitted by fingers.

- **Fingertips.** Agorithms are derived from measurements of an individual's fingertip shape and texture.

- **Hand geometry/image.** An electronic scan of a person's hand is made first, then a three-dimensional image is generated. Ninety different aspects of the hand are measured, including width, depth, shape of the fingers, and size of knuckles. These are compared to a previous scan of the person that provided a reference profile. The encoded profile data are stored either in computer memory, on a magnetic stripe, or in a smart card. A positive match between the current hand scan and stored data allows access. Another method takes a digital picture of the inside of a person's hand via an infrared scanner.

- **Iris recognition.** The iris is the colored ring pattern around the pupil of the eye. A scanning device measures and analyzes the unique color patterns of the iris, then takes a video picture of the iris, which is converted into a digital code that can be compared. The iris has approximately 266 measurable characteristics, and the pattern is relatively stable over time and aging.

- **Keystroke dynamics.** This technique measures the speed and pattern of keystroke entry by an individual. In the early 1990s this system showed some promise. Since then other biometric systems have gained more acceptance because they are more accurate, easier to use, and less intrusive.

- **Retinal patterns.** This system recognizes an individual by the retinal vessel pattern of the eye. A scanned reference picture is stored in a computer as a standard for comparison and matching.

- **Signature dynamics.** Automated signature verification systems are based on the dynamics of the signer's pen motion related to time. The measurements are signature shape, speed, stroke, pen pressure, angle of the pen, and timing, taken via a digitized tablet. A signer is enrolled by taking three or more measurements of his or her signature; an average figure is obtained and stored in the computer. Future signatures are compared with the average figure.

- **Voice verification.** "Prints" of a person's voice can be recorded in an analog signal, which is converted to digital. A set of measurements is derived and stored in a computer. The references are based on an individual's vocal pattern by speaking several single words. The system may require an individual to say three words out of a reference file of seven. A match of the words spoken with those on file allows access.

Newer systems record voice frequency every one-hundredth of a second and generate a three-dimensional image representing the sound a voice produces in one second. Systems can measure and compare unique vocal characteristics such as pitch, tone, and cadence.

SMART CARDS AND PORTABLE DATA CARRIERS

A smart card functions as a portable database. Its most common form resembles a standard credit card, but it can also be configured like a token, a key, a military ID tag, a personal identification badge, or in any other shape required. The card allows information to be accessed and retrieved via a card reader connected to a personal computer, "dumb" terminal, automatic teller machine, point-of-sale terminal, telephone, electronic lock, or any number of other devices.

Software resides in the reader and is also located on the card in the form of integrated circuit chips. The function of the reader is to detect the presence of a card and to provide a standard interface so that the card can communicate with and access different hosts, including a remote server or specific sections of a network and specific data files. Host computers or terminals can interact with the smart card using predefined software commands. Communication can be via the Internet or a wireless transmitter.

With faster processors and more memory, a smart card can support multiple independent applications on one card. Authentication/verification, encryption, nonrepudiation, and other security can be built in. It is possible to digitize hand-written signatures, fingerprints, and voiceprints or other personal biometric identifiers and store them on the card for later comparison with those of the user. Each data file stored in the card can be assigned its own security level, with separate read and write permissions.

Smart cards have become multitechnology devices that can provide access control, encryption, and electronic signatures necessary to secure personal information. Vendors of smart cards, tokens, and keys include Litronic, Verisign, American Biometric, Schlumberger Smart Cards & Terminals North America, Krypton Software, ActivCard S.A., Oberthur Smart Cards, Passlogix, Spyrus, Bull Worldwide Information Systems, Gemplus, Datacard, VASCO Data Security, Datakey, PubliCARD, Racal Security Payments, Cardlogix, Entrust, First Access, CryptoCard, and Cylink.

POSSIBLE DIRECTIONS AND DEVELOPMENTS IN BIOMETRICS

In access control one can see total systems coming together: automated identification, data capture and storage, and data communications. Biometrics will be merged with other access control IDs such as barcodes, magnetic stripes, and smart cards.

Biometrics used as a personal identifier may not be too far away. The hunt for a single identifier will be replaced by "layering": face and voice, or fingerprint and signature. Identification technology and management is taking shape at the federal and state levels in areas such as tracking individuals at borders and airports, driver's licenses, secure patient records, benefits IDs, fraud control, and blood donation. (For more on the uses of biometrics in e-business, see Chapter 10.)

CONCERNS ABOUT BIOMETRIC SYSTEMS

Having systems make and store digital records of personal biological information seems to some people to be personally invasive and raises concerns about privacy and security.

Biometric devices give rise to fears that scanning body parts might give organizations opportunities to learn more about their customers than they have the right to know, such as health, race, and disabilities. Users are not necessarily protected from organizations selling the biometric data to third parties. There is also a question of ownership and control of the biometric information, including who can share biometric information. Some wonder whether the use of biometrics in transactions could mean more convenience, lower costs, and better protection of the consumer's money. But there is also concern about the level of transaction at which biometrics is really needed.

SELECTING A BIOMETRIC SYSTEM

The first question you should ask when considering installing a biometrics system is: "Are biometrics really needed at this level of transaction?" Even if the answer is "yes," there are unique problems associated with selecting a biometric security system. Following are basic questions to ask vendors:

- How stable or reliable is the biometric attribute itself?

- What can affect the system? (Include the percentage of the population that lacks the identifying attribute, such as having no fingers, being unable to speak, or having glaucoma.)

- How accurate is the measurement of the biometric?

- What is the system's storage capacity for biometric data?

- What is the throughput or operating speed of the system?

- What is the average enrollment time for users?

- Is the system too technical for your operation or use?

- Is the biometric identifier too intrusive or invasive, raising possible liability in making and storing biological details about a person? What further "evidence" can be gleaned from biometric data?

- How easy is it for the system to be "layered" with another biometric or ID?

- What are the costs of the system for hardware, software, installation, training, maintenance, and so forth?

- How easy is it to merge with information or physical security systems? Is an applications programming software interface available?

- How reliable is the biometrics system? What tests, including beta testing, have been done on it? (The vendor should also be able to supply information on lab tests of biometric systems; Sandia Labs, to name one, has performed tests for government agencies.)

- Does the technology require little effort on the part of the consumer; that is, is it user-friendly?

- Has this system had broad usage? If yes, in what context: military/governmen, private industry, or consumer? How did the system fare? What other use tests have been done?

- Is there a compatible backup system for the particular biometric product?

- Is there a training program for potential users on the system, covering such things as device/system operations, personal interaction, and ergonomics?

- Can you supply information on error rates for false rejections (false rejection of authorized personnel) and false acceptances (admission of an imposter)? (For high security, a very low false acceptance rate is important. Where authorized personnel should be allowed access with a minimum of inconvenience, a low false rejection rate is desirable. Although equipment can be adjusted to modify error rates, it is necessary always to keep in mind the security objective for the specific access control point or object.)

Preparing a table to rate comparable access control systems can help you in decision making. You can rate types of systems or specific manufacturers. To set up a table, place the systems or brands of access control in a left-hand column. Put evaluation categories across the top of the table. The categories chosen will depend on what is most important and unique to your organization. Following are some basic categories to consider:

- lowest procurement cost

- the costs of changing the ID, such as personal passwords, over a time period

- lowest average monthly cost

- best employee acceptance

- best visitor acceptance

- greatest compatibility with security operations and personnel

- ease of installation

- ease of operation, including ID changes

- most workable software

- reliability of system operation

- vendor warranty

- technical training and support from vendor

- highest level of security

- insurance carrier preference

- compliance with regulatory/legal/government contract requirements

BIOMETRIC PRODUCTS AND VENDORS

Table 11.1 lists suppliers of various biometric security systems.

Application programming interface software can be obtained from Keyware Technologies, Unisys, Microsoft, Novell, Visionics, Silanis Technology, Valicert, Acumen Data Systems, and Microsystems.

TABLE 11.1   Biometric Products and Vendors

Type of Product	Vendors
Facial recognition	Visionics Corp., Miros, Inc., NeuroMetric Vision Systems, Viisage Technology, Diebold, NCR, Keyware Technologies, CashAmerica International
Finger image	Identicator Technology, Control Module, Unisys, HID Corp.
Fingerprint	Biometric Identification, Identix, AuthenTec, Digital Biometrics, Key Trak, NEC Technologies, Mytec Technologies, Motorola Imaging Systems, Key Tronic, Sony, American Biometric, Veridicom
Hand geometry/image	Recognition Systems, Konetix, Advanced Biometrics
Iris recognition	IriScan, Sensar/Iridian Technologies
Key stroke dynamics	International Biometric Systems
Retinal scan	Eyedentify
Signature dynamics	Digital Signature, CyberSign, Inc., Noetel, LCI Technology Group, PenOp, Communication Intelligence, Interlink Electronics, CyberSafe
Voice verification	Thorn Automated Systems, Voice Sciences, Veritel, Keyware Technologies, Verbex Voice Systems, and Kurzweil

12

ENCRYPTION SECURITY FOR ELECTRONIC COMMERCE

One of the means by which electronic commerce takes place is through Electronic Data Interchange (EDI). Until recently, if a company wanted to take advantage of EDI, the setup required an expensive investment in hardware and software. Today, small businesses can take advantage of a value-added network (VAN) or Internet-based EDI. The Internet allows companies to exchange ordering, shipping, payment, and inventory information. A VAN is usually offered by a large company to smaller companies without full EDI capabilities. However, Web/Internet-based EDI is becoming the vehicle of choice for most small businesses. Another Internet option is a virtual private network (VPN), which is a collection of technologies that provide secure "tunnels" over Internet lines. A VPN can provide site-to-site connectivity and security features such as firewalls, compression, encryption (discussed below), authentication, and public key exchanges (discussed below). VPN technologies are available for Windows NT and UNIX.

EDI is the automated exchange of structured business data, such as invoices, purchase orders, and other documents and forms, via computer, between businesses. Financial EDI is the exchange of payment information—credit or debit instructions—through a banking system's automated clearinghouse or certain VANs. Usually these EDI instructions, documents, or payments are separate exchanges of financial and nonfinancial data, depending on networks, VANs, and banks.

An EDI information exchange is based primarily on a contract. If a set of promises is broken, there is a legal remedy. This means that trading partner agreements can include descriptions of forms and documents; payment terms; delivery schedules; and specific control, security, and audit measures. The American Bar Association has issued a "Model Trading Partner Agreement" that defines terms of acceptance and allows for adoption by parties of electronic signatures ("symbols or codes which are to be affixed to or contained in each document transmitted by such party;" see Chapter 10), encryption, and other security measures.

All contracts for the sale of goods over $500 come under Uniform Commercial Code (U.C.C.) § 2-201, the Statute of Frauds. This section requires that the contract be in a "writing" and that it be "signed" by the party. To meet the requirements of § 2-201, the writing must evidence a contract for the sale of goods, be signed in a way that authenticates and identifies the party to be charged, and specify the quantity. A complete signature to authenticate a writing is not necessary: "Authentication may be printed, stamped, or written; it may be by initials or by thumbprint. It may be on any part of the document and in appropriate cases may be found in a billhead or letterhead." A digital signature may provide the authentication needed for a party to satisfy this section. Encryption is a vital security method for the transmission or storage of the signature.

SECURITY RISKS IN EDI

EDI presents some risks that are significantly different from those of a standalone computer or a dedicated system. Once outside access is permitted, a risk assessment should be done of the host system's security. The basic concerns here are threats such as data system destruction and damage, data disclosure and modification, processing delays, and denial of service. Backup and recovery should receive critical scrutiny.

To maximize its cost-reduction capabilities, EDI creates many databases, accessible by many people for many purposes. Typical access control features for individual EDI users include terminal and user IDs, user behavior characteristics and normal patterns of use, and user authorization limits. These control measures are intended to restrict access to those persons with preestablished needs and to limit even those persons to data that are vital to the proper discharge of their job-related duties. The controls are intended to monitor, flag, and log exceptions and security rules.

SECURE ONLINE CONSUMER PAYMENT SYSTEMS

Commerce on the Internet has spawned a number of different ways for consumers to order products and pay for them. With security perceived as a major problem when exposing credit card information, several systems have been proposed. More will be developed as the private sector leads the way in technology solutions for securing electronic transactions. One type of secure payment system takes the customer's financial information off-line, encrypts it, and never displays it live on the Internet. The most common encryption method is the Data Encryption Standard (DES). Another is public key encryption. Other software applications may use a Graphics User Interface (GUI) keypad, employing proprietary algorithms that randomly encrypt numbers, for example those on a credit card, then send the numbers one at a time. Another method gives "digital certificates" to online banks, merchants, and consumers. The certificates can include Personal Identification Numbers (PINs), an authentication mechanism, and encryption.

A number of transaction security methods have been developed, including Secure Electronic Transactions (SET), which is a set of protocols developed by MasterCard and Visa; Secure Electronic Payment Protocol Specification (SEPP); and Secure Sockets Layer (SSL), supported by Netscape's browser Navigator.

DATA ENCRYPTION

Encryption is the other half of a secure electronic communication system. It ensures that the message was transmitted by an authenticated sender to the authorized receiver without being opened. The National Bureau of Standard's Data Encryption Standard (DES) was developed to safeguard sensitive but unclassified federal computerized data. It is also available to nonfederal organizations. The DES was first published in 1977.

The DES is a series of mathematical steps (an algorithm) applied to human-readable data to make them unintelligible (encrypted). The same mathematical steps are then applied in reverse order to the unintelligible data to make them readable again (decrypted). If the mathematical steps were the only components of the encryption/decryption process, a diligent thief could break the code. The DES, therefore, provides the user with an eight-character key that can be changed.

The mathematical algorithm for the DES consists of permutations and substitutions with iterations of these functions to complete the process. A *permutation* is generally a rearranging of the bits of a piece of data, including the addition or subtraction of bits to the original data, without changing the value of the bits. A substitution, on the other hand, does not necessarily preserve the value of bits.

Once the eight-character keys have been established, the actual data are passed through the encryption algorithm. The data are divided into eight character pieces to be processed. These characters are transformed into their eight-bit representations, resulting in a 64-bit string of 1s and 0s. This string is then passed through an initial permutation. The 64-bit output of the permutation is then passed through 16 iterations of a complex substitution process. Once these 16 iterations are complete, a final permutation, an inverse of the initial permutation, is performed to produce the final encrypted data output. When the data are to be deciphered, the entire process is reversed.

The heart of the DES is the algorithms, but successful implementation is based on the key that is used in the encryption/decryption process. Both the sender and the receiver must have the same key. The security of the transmitted data depends not only on the DES but also on the keys being kept secure. The proper management of key selection, security, and distribution are critical to successful implementation of a DES-based system.

Triple DES (128-bit) is a recent standard. The Commerce Department approved finding an encryption technique for a Federal Information Processing Standard (FIPS) for an Advanced Encryption Standard (AES) incorporating an Advanced Encryption Algorithm (AEA) in 1997. FIPS 196 is for federal agencies and specifies an "unclassified, publicly disclosed encryption algorithm capable of protecting sensitive government information," using a public key cryptography.

The minimum requirements for the Triple DES are that it be publicly defined, a symmetric block cipher, designed so that the key length may be increased as needed, implementable in both hardware and software, and either freely available or available under terms consistent with the American National Standards Institute patent policy. Algorithms that meet the above requirements will be judged for security (the effort required to cryptanalyze), computational efficiency, memory requirements, hardware and software suitability, simplicity, flexibility, and licensing requirements. In October 2000, the Commerce Department endorsed "Rijndael," an encryption algorithm created by two Belgian computer scientists.

PUBLIC KEY SYSTEMS

Another encryption methodology uses public keys. The encryption algorithm depends not on one key that both parties must know, but on two keys. One, a public key, which scrambles a message, is made available to anyone who wants to send information to a given person. The second key is a private key, known only to the owner, and is needed to unscramble the message. The private key is not easily derived from the public key.

The RSA algorithm (1024-bit) is based on keys determined by factoring a very large number (200 digits) into its primes. The public key is used in simple mathematical functions against the data to be transmitted, but the private key is needed to decrypt the message.

Keeping track of and securing encryption keys can be handled by a company internally or be turned over to a third party. For public keys, there is a certificate authority (CA), which can issue digital certificates assuring the validity of a key. This is like an access control process of identifying and verifying the person or device seeking to communicate across a network. Besides managing the certificate and its key, a CA may also manage a directory of stored certificates, provide a revocation system to stop use of a certificate, renew certificates, assure the nonrepudiation of a key, and provide means for key backup and recovery.

To manage the huge number of digital certificates and to promote e-commerce growth, a public key infrastructure (PKI) may be needed. A PKI is a digital certificate system of validated private and public key pairs involved in an Internet transaction. Browser and other software applications are offering what is essentially a "PKI package" of key management capabilities from signing, verification, encryption/decryption, revocation, and directories of certificates, along with means for key backup and recovery.

Privacy and security are vital to the creation of trust and confidence in an e-business. This holds true whether the company operates for business-to-consumer or business-to-business. A company must protect the privacy of information entrusted to it by consumers or trading partners.

13

PROTECTING PROPRIETARY INFORMATION

Management attaches importance to proprietary information. Intellectual property has legal status and thus a higher recognition. But not all important information is necessarily given this recognition at its birth. Much of it is in a state of becoming, not yet given the status of a proprietary or an intellectual property niche. When information reaches the stage where it is seen as having value or potential value as an intangible asset that can contribute to the enterprise's earning power, it deserves protection. A key fact to keep in mind is that losing rights to business information is just like losing money. (For more on the connection between e-business and protecting proprietary information, see Chapter 10.)

To be protected as a trade secret information must be novel; that is, it cannot exist in the public domain. However, the information that is not unique can be combined in such a way as to make it new and different and possibly qualify for trade secret protection. A trade secret is "any information that can be used in the operation of a business that is sufficiently valuable and secret to afford an actual or potential economic advantage over others" (*Restatement of the Law Third*, Unfair Competition).

For confidential information to be given the legal status of a trade secret, it must be commercial information. That is, it cannot be just any information that a firm does not want known, such as an internal report that discloses poor management practices. The commercial information must have a value that lies in the competitive advantage it gives over business rivals. Another essential element of a trade secret is its confidential nature, which must be maintained.

PROTECTING PROPRIETARY INFORMATION

The Economic Espionage Act of 1996 (Public Law 104-294) provides a broad definition of a trade secret:

> The term "trade secret" means all forms and types of financial, business, scientific, technical, economic, or engineering information, including patterns, plans, compilations, program devices, formulas, designs, prototypes, methods, techniques, processes, procedures, programs or codes, whether tangible or intangible, and whether or how stored, compiled or memorialized physically, electronically, graphically, photographically, or in writing.

Information that could be a candidate for trade secret status is often created, manipulated, and stored on a computer. An example is market research data. As it is collected in raw form, such as survey questionnaire tabulations, it may not meet the requirements for being a trade secret, but it would certainly require being protected as proprietary information. The methodology used, such as a proprietary survey sampling technique, or the mailing list, if compiled in-house using customer names, should qualify as a trade secret. The elements used in a marketing research survey—the research methodology, the survey select sample, and the statistical analysis—may be commonly known. However, the combination of these elements can result in marketing information or a plan that qualifies as a trade secret.

Other marketing, sales, and promotion information that deserves protection includes consumer or customer names, purchasing habits, and demographics; marketing research plans or strategies; customer lists; sales methods; order fulfillment procedures and systems; and product pricing. Additional candidates for protection are business information on contracts or agreements with affiliated companies, vendors, subcontractors, and consultants.

The two major elements of a trade secret are being novel (not in the public domain) and conferring a commercially competitive advantage, or potential advantage, to its owner. The novelty of the plan or one of its elements is not necessarily critical to trade secret status; if the totality of the plan

146

is unique in that everything about it is not common industry knowledge, and the marketing plan confers a competitive advantage, the information is a trade secret.

Trade secret law and policies can create a framework for internal controls that may ensure the confidentiality, privacy, and security of information, be it trade secrets, proprietary information, or personal "nonpublic" information. Protection measures such as policies, agreements, and security have a strong legal mandate. Legal sanctions for misappropriation can be invoked swiftly and precisely.

TRADE SECRET VALUE AND EXPLOITATION

The essence of a trade secret is that it has value. Its ultimate value occurs when it finds the highest and best use, yielding the greatest return through exploitation either within the enterprise or by transferring rights to others via licensing and royalty arrangements. Assigning a final value to trade secret information may be impossible given the many, often subtle, permutations of valuation. One thing is sure: An unused trade secret could be called worthless.

Before it can be exploitable, trade secret information is in a stage of becoming. The potential is visible, but the "package" isn't ready. At this stage, the element of "reasonable and obvious" security enters, along with some recordkeeping, bookkeeping, and legal issues. Recordkeeping must start with identifying the information to be protected, retaining all the related documentation during development, and making sure all documents are signed and dated. Bookkeeping should be not only a record of costs (time, effort, and expense) for information development, but also of the costs of protection. All records, including electronic ones, should be created and maintained to meet the business records standard under Federal Rule of Evidence 803(6).

Protection and value of trade secret information are joined in a series of cost-benefit analyses. This fact implies the use of periodic, focused audits of trade secret programs to monitor development, value, and protection compliance.

TRADE SECRETS CAN LOSE CONFIDENTIALITY

Outside parties can discover a company's trade secrets through

- independent invention,

- reverse engineering,

- observation of the item in public use or on public display,

- obtaining the information from public literature, and

- carelessness in handling or in security procedures.

The clearest way to abandon secrecy is to make public disclosure of the information. This does not necessarily mean broad public dissemination; telling a single third party will suffice as long as it is not done in confidence. A patent issuance will end trade secret status. The age or relevance of the information can also affect its trade secret status.

TRADE SECRETS AND
INTELLECTUAL PROPERTY LAW

Technological and business information that is used secretly inside a company, lends a competitive advantage, and is not known generally by competitors, is legally protectable as a trade secret. What is considered protectable as a trade secret includes varieties of information for which patent protection may not be available. The U.S. Supreme Court has ruled that trade secret law is independent of and complementary to the patent system (see *Gottschalk v. Benson*, 409 U.S. 63 (1972)). For many types of technological information, such as complex industrial processes and formulas, trade secrets and patents are alternative forms of protection. Other innovative matter, such as computer software and related developments, may be only marginally protectable by patent or copyright and are better protected as trade secrets.

A company can seek patent protection for computer software *or* retain the matter as a trade secret. A patent protects any new or useful process, machine, manufacture, or composition of matter, or any new and useful improvement. A computer program is a process or an integral part of a machine, and is therefore patentable. In January 1999, the Supreme Court, in *State St. Bank & Trust v. Signature Financial Group,* ruled that a patent can cover digital business processes. It is too early to determine how Internet business method patents will fare. However, the scope of what can be patented is expanding rapidly.

Trade secret law is generally based on common law and contractual provisions. Although patents and copyrights fall under federal law, the law of each state defines what a trade secret is, the rights of the holder, and the enforcement of all trade secret claims. State trade secret law is not preempted by federal law. Unlike patent or copyright, there is no limit on the duration of a trade secret. The Trade Secrets Act of 1996 (18 U.S.C. 1905) prohibits unauthorized release of any information relating to trade secrets or confidential business information by a federal officer or employee.

Elements of Trade Secret Law

In 1979 the Uniform Trade Secrets Act (UTSA) was approved by the National Conference of Commissioners on Uniform State Laws. It was amended in 1985. UTSA, which has been adopted, with variations, into the civil codes of more than 30 states, gives the following definition of a trade secret:

> "Trade secret" means information, including a formula, pattern, compilation, program, device, method, technique, or process that:

> (i). derives independent economic value, actual or potential, from not being generally known to, and not being readily ascertainable by proper means, by other persons who can obtain economic value from its disclosure or use, and

> (ii). is the subject of efforts that are reasonable under the circumstances to maintain its secrecy.

Tort Law Protection for Trade Secrets

A trade secret becomes property to be protected, as another asset of the firm. The *Restatement of Torts,* (Section 757) contains clarification of factors to be considered in determining whether information can be a secret:

1. The extent to which the information is known outside of the business;

2. The extent to which it is known by employees and others involved in the business;

3. The extent of measures taken by the business to guard the secrecy of the information;

4. The value of the information to the business and its competitors;

5. The amount of effort or money expended by the business in developing the information; and,

6. The ease or difficulty with which the information could be properly acquired or duplicated by others.

Misappropriation of Trade Secrets

To establish a claim of misappropriation of a trade secret, the *Restatement* requires that

1. There must be a protectable interest, i.e., a trade secret;

2. The plaintiff must have a proprietary interest in the trade secret;

3. The trade secret must be disclosed to the defendant in confidence or it must be wrongfully acquired by the defendant through improper means;

4. There must be a duty not to use or disclose the information; and,

5. There must be a likely or past disclosure or use of the information, if in a different form, which is unfair or inequitable to the plaintiff.

150

The statutory definition of misappropriation states that no person, including the government, may misappropriate or threaten to misappropriate a trade secret by:

a. acquiring the trade secret of another by means which the person knows or has reason to know constitute improper means;

b. disclosing or using without express or implied consent a trade secret of another if the person did any of the following:

   (i). used improper means to acquire knowledge of the trade secret;

   (ii). at the time of disclosure or use, knew or had reason to know that he or she obtained knowledge of the trade secret through any of the following means:

      a. deriving it from or through a person who utilized improper means to acquire it;

      b. acquiring it under circumstances giving rise to a duty to maintain its secrecy or limit its use;

      c. deriving it from or through a person who owed a duty to the person seeking relief to maintain its secrecy or limit its use;

      d. acquiring it by accident or mistake.

The phrase "improper means" has been defined in the Uniform Trade Secrets Act to include espionage, theft, bribery, misrepresentation, and breach or inducement of a breach of duty to maintain secrecy.

Remedies for misappropriation of trade secrets include injunction, actual and punitive damages, and attorney fees. State statutes covering trade secret theft usually contain criminal sanctions.

Injunctive Remedies   As soon as a trade secret misappropriation is discovered, the company should ask the court for a temporary restraining order or preliminary injunction to prevent disclosure of trade secrets. This forces the offender to immediately cease violating a confidentiality agreement. The company must be ready to demonstrate to the court the value of the information and the damage the enterprise will suffer if the trade secret information is disseminated or misused. An injunction should last for a reasonable period of time to prevent commercial advantage to the violator.

Recovery for Damages   In addition to, or instead of, injunctive relief, courts may award damages. For trade secret misappropriation by employees, compensatory or money damages can be recovered. In determining damages, the court may examine the trade secret owner's loss, the defendant's gain, or both. Knowing the fact of damage caused by the loss of a trade secret is the critical first step. The next step is to determine and show the amount of damages. This can mean both actual loss and any unjust enrichment to the defendant(s).

Actual loss can be documented by showing the labor and money spent in the creation of the thing being misappropriated. Competition by the company or person who took the product results in commercial damage to the plaintiff. Punitive damages may also be awarded if the defendant's conduct was "willful and malicious misappropriation" of the owner's trade secret.

The body of trade secret cases relevant to information systems has grown steadily. One of the most prominent cases is *Telex Corp. v. IBM* (1975), in which IBM recovered $23 million from Telex for theft of IBM product development material. There have been numerous prosecutions for theft of computer programs and software.

Economic Espionage Act

The Economic Espionage Act of 1996 (Public Law 104-294) is designed to protect proprietary economic information. It creates criminal penalties for the theft; unauthorized appropriation or conversion, duplication, alteration, or destruction; or wrongful copying or control of trade secrets, or the wrongful diversion of a trade secret to benefit someone other than its owners or create some disadvantage to the rightful owners. The act amends Title 18 of the U.S. Code by inserting a new chapter, 90. Section 1831 of chapter 90 prohibits anyone from obtaining trade secrets by fraud, theft, or deception for the benefit of a foreign agent or government. Violators who are individuals can be fined up to $500,000 and imprisoned for up to 15 years; organizations can be fined up to $10 million.

The term *wrongful* involves

> the defendant's knowledge that his or her actions in copying or otherwise exerting control over the information in question was inappropriate. It is not necessary that the government prove that the defendant knew his or her actions were illegal, rather the government must prove that the defendant's actions were not authorized by the nature of his or her relationship to the owner of the property and that the defendant knew or should have known that fact.

Under the act, the government must prove that the defendant acted with "the intent to, or with reason to believe that the offense would, benefit any foreign government, foreign instrumentality, or foreign agent." The act calls for a broad definition of *benefit* that goes beyond a strictly economic advantage, also conferring a "reputational, strategic, or tactical benefit."

The act seeks to punish methods of misappropriation or destruction that involve duplication or alteration: "When these non-traditional methods are used the original property never leaves the control of the rightful owner, but the unauthorized duplication or misappropriation effectively destroys the value of what is left with the rightful owner." Information can be stolen from computer systems without being "carried off" as defined in traditional theft statutes: "It is the intent of this statute to ensure that the theft of intangible information is prohibited in the same way that the theft of physical items is punished."

Receiving, buying, or possessing a trade secret known to be stolen is an offense. Attempts to steal, or conspiracies to steal, trade secrets are also prohibited. A *trade secret* is defined as "all forms and types of financial, business, scientific, technical, economic, or engineering information" having independent economic value, and for which the owner has "taken reasonable measures to keep such information secret." A determination of the "reasonableness of the steps taken by the owner to keep the information secret will vary from case to case and be dependent upon the nature of the information in question."

Under Section 1832 of the act, it is an offense to convert a trade secret that is related to or a part of a product in interstate or foreign commerce if the trade secret was obtained without authorization or through theft. It is also illegal for anyone, without authorization from the owner, to make copies of trade secret information, communicate such information, receive or buy, or attempt or conspire to do any of these things if doing so would cause injury to the trade secret owner. Conviction carries a fine or imprisonment of not more than 10 years, or both. Organizations can be fined not more than $5 million.

The statute includes a criminal forfeiture provision in addition to any other sentence. Any property or proceeds derived from the crime, or property used or intended to be used in the crime, may be forfeited.

Congress intends this act to help federal law enforcement agencies combat trade secret thefts by foreign companies, often with the cooperation of foreign governments, as well as thefts by U.S. employees. Before this law there was no federal criminal statute that dealt directly with economic espionage or the protection of proprietary economic information. Under existing law, there is no statutory procedure to protect the victim's stolen information during criminal proceedings. However, in any prosecution or proceeding, a court may issue orders to preserve the confidentiality of trade secrets. In a civil action, the attorney general may issue injunctive relief against any violation under the Economic Espionage Act.

National Stolen Property Act

The National Stolen Property Act of 1996 (18 U.S.C. 2314) calls for criminal sanctions against any person who "transports, transmits, or transfers in interstate or foreign commerce any goods, wares, merchandise, securities or money, of the value of $5,000 or more, knowing the same to have been stolen, converted or taken by fraud." Penalties can be a fine of up to $10,000, a prison sentence of 10 years, or both.

The aim of the statute is to prohibit the use of interstate transportation facilities to move stolen goods and to punish theft of property when such punishment is beyond the capability of an individual state. Therefore, the "movement" of a trade secret across state lines must be established (see *U.S. v. Riggs*) Also, it must be established that the defendant had knowledge that the information was property and that it was stolen.

To get a conviction under this statute,

- the items must be transported or transmitted in interstate or foreign commerce;

- the items must meet the definition of goods, wares, merchandise, securities, or money;

- the items—property or money—must have a value of $5,000 or more;

- the defendant must have knowledge that the items were stolen or falsely made; and

- the items must have been stolen, converted, or taken by fraudulent means.

Federal courts have ruled that confidential information stored on a computer is valuable property under the definition of "goods, wares, or merchandise." A person who "transmitted" stolen proprietary business information from one computer to another across state lines can be prosecuted under this statute.

Various federal laws also come into play when stolen information is transferred or transmitted. First are the wire or mail fraud statutes. These statutes are often merged with or underlie a charge of conspiracy. These laws are discussed below.

INTERNATIONAL PROTECTIONS FOR TRADE SECRETS

Protection of trade secrets (called "undisclosed information") in all GATT (General Agreement on Tariffs and Trade) countries is covered in Article 39. Natural as well as legal persons may prevent information being disclosed to, acquired by, or used by others without their consent as long as the information is relatively secret, has commercial value because it is secret, and has been the subject of reasonable efforts to keep it secret.

The North American Free Trade Agreement (NAFTA), which came into effect in 1995, uses the broader phrase "actual or potential" commercial value (17, Article 1711(1)(b)). A gross negligence standard is established for disclosure of trade secrets to third parties. NAFTA's provisions offer stronger protection for U.S. intellectual property than does GATT.

CHECKLIST OF BASIC PROPRIETARY INFORMATION PROTECTION MEASURES

Proprietary confidential information is seldom static; technology and service product lifecycles have shrunk, often to less than two years. Protective measures must be as dynamic as the confidential information. Use the following checklist to implement adequate measures to protect proprietary information.

- ❑ Advise employees of the existence of trade secrets in the company.

- ❑ Keep records of the time and investment required to create trade secret information.

- ❑ Identify by name and position all persons to whom trade secret information was disclosed.

- ❑ Make access to trade secrets strictly on a "need to know" basis.

CHECKLIST OF BASIC PROPRIETARY INFORMATION PROTECTION

❏ Use risk and vulnerability analyses to determine the threat of loss of trade secret information.

❏ Implement internal controls and physical security measures that are obvious, reasonable, and adequate.

❏ Keep records of the costs of protecting trade secrets.

❏ Document and periodically audit all protective measures.

❏ Recognize that trade secret protection is an ongoing program of cost/benefit analysis. Protection should be adequate to threat and value.

❏ Confidentiality/secrecy agreements should be specific in terms of individual, information, location, and time/duration. A covenant not to disclose secrets and an agreement to report any unauthorized disclosures should be included in such agreements. Company-wide trade secret statements will likely be inadequate.

❏ Affected employees should be required to sign confidentiality agreements.

14

SECRECY AND NONCOMPETE AGREEMENTS

A secrecy/confidentiality agreement is a way for a company to keep its technical, business, or proprietary information confidential and private. These agreements create a confidential relationship with either an employee or someone outside the company, such as a supplier, subcontractor, or employees of an affiliated company. They are used for securing secrecy and privacy with respect to inventions, technical information, know-how, trade secrets, and other confidential proprietary information. A secrecy/confidentiality agreement is a key element in an overall company program of intellectual property and proprietary information protection. A trade secret or confidentiality clause should be part of agreements with employees, independent contractors or consultants, vendors, distributors, lenders, partners, and shareholders.

A signed secrecy/confidentiality agreement is necessary to create or preserve intellectual property protection rights. Where the employee is provided access to trade secret information through a computer, the company may first insert a computer screen that puts the employee on notice that information he or she is about to access is proprietary and requires the employee to enter a response acknowledging the protected status of the information.

Secrecy/confidentiality agreements should not be entered into casually and without legal advice or assistance. Although there is a common law obligation on employees not to disclose or use their current or former employer's trade secrets, and a fiduciary duty for officers, a signed agreement is evidence of an employer's intention to protect trade secrets and proprietary information.

ELEMENTS OF A SECRECY/CONFIDENTIALITY AGREEMENT

Secrecy/confidentiality agreements should cover

- The employee you want to enter into an agreement.

- The divisions, departments, or subunits of the company involved.

- The location where the affected activity is likely to be performed (e.g., in which state of the United States).

- A description of trade secrets and the trade secret or confidential information the employee has access to. This should be a broad definition that covers paper and electronic documents as well as copies of materials. Indicate the particular product(s), activity, or manufacturing process to which the information relates as well as the kind of information (e.g., software, designs, quality assurance reports, marketing data or reports, consumer data, test market specifications, computer programs).

- Whether trade secret information will be physically identified/marked or verbally identified to the employee.

- When or for how long the information is to be available to the employee.

- The fact that the company is protecting its trade secret or proprietary information.

- Stipulations that the employee will not disclose or misappropriate trade secret or proprietary information during or subsequent to employment, and that continued employment with the company is contigent upon compliance with the secrecy/confidentiality agreement.

- A requirement that the employee will report any unauthorized disclosure or use of trade secret or proprietary information.

- The period of time during which the employee is to keep the information in confidence. (Be specific).

- The fact that the proprietary information and trade secrets are created at substantial cost to the company and that disclosure would cause great harm to the company.

- A provision that, if action is taken against misappropriation by an employee and injunctive relief is sought, there will be an agreed-upon amount of bond or security to protect the employee against whom the injunction may be issued.

POINTS TO REMEMBER ABOUT SECRECY/CONFIDENTIALITY AGREEMENTS

Keep the following in mind when entering into secrecy/confidentiality agreements:

- Secrecy/confidentiality agreements must be reasonable in scope and not contrary to public policy.

- Only top management should be authorized to enter into and sign secrecy agreements.

- Secrecy/confidentiality agreements are enforceable, and injunctions may be granted and large damages awarded for not adhering to them.

- Avoid disclosing trade secret information to any outsider except under an enforceable secrecy agreement.

- Consult with legal counsel before entering into any and all secrecy/confidentiality agreements.

SECRECY/CONFIDENTIALITY AGREEMENTS WITH VENDORS, AFFILIATES, OR OTHER THIRD PARTIES

Secrecy/confidentiality agreements with parties outside the company should include the following information:

- Name and address (city, county, state, and state of incorporation) of company or individuals you want to enter into an agreement with.

- The specific information to be provided to the parties (be as specific here as with an employee agreement).

- What specific use the parties will make of the proprietary information.

- When the parties will receive the information.

- For what period of time the parties must keep the information confidential.

- A provision for the recovery of legal fees by your company.

NONCOMPETE AGREEMENTS

Companies should provide notice of postemployment nondisclosure. This may be a separate agreement in the form of a restrictive covenant, which is a provision reasonably restricting competition by the employee after his or her employment is finished. It should not be too broad regarding time, territory, or activities. The enforcement of restrictive covenants varies from state to state, so they must be carefully drafted to conform with a particular state's laws.

When drafting noncompete agreements, keep the following guidelines in mind:

- Non-compete agreements should be made with all employees who have knowledge of or access to trade secrets or confidential proprietary information that would be damaging in the hands of a competitor.

- To be enforceable, a promise not to compete must be given in exchange for adequate consideration. If the covenant is part of the employment contract before hiring, the job offer can be the "consideration." Prior to hiring is a good time to give the employee a copy of the agreement to review. For a current employee a "sufficient consideration" could be additional benefits received.

- Noncompete agreements should be entered into only if necessary for the protection of the employer's legitimate business interests, which include trade secrets and confidential proprietary information.

- Provide a reasonable time restriction, usually defined as no longer than necessary to protect the employer's interests. Barring anyone from practicing his or her trade for three years would most likely be an unacceptable restriction. Another means of deciding how long a restriction to request is how long it may take to replace and retrain a new employee.

- Provide a reasonable territorial limit, an area not broader than the employer's protectable interest, such as service to customers. The employer must demonstrate that the restriction is necessary to protect the business.

- A noncompete agreement cannot be contrary to public policy, such as limiting competition or forcing the employee to go on public assistance.

- A noncompete agreement should not be harsh or oppressive to the employee; the burden on the employee must be as light as possible. The employer must be willing to post a bond or give the employee severance pay for not competing with the company.

ENFORCING A SECRECY/CONFIDENTIALITY AGREEMENT

Take the following steps to enforce an agreement that it appears has not been complied with:

- Notify the employee (or third parties) demanding compliance with the confidentiality agreement.

- File a lawsuit immediately to prevent disclosure of trade secret information and qualify for injunctive relief.

- Begin an internal investigation to determine whether the employee has compromised or stole proprietary information.

- Conduct an interview with the employee (if possible) about his or her new employment, employer, job duties and responsibilities, contacts with your company's customers, and whether he or she has taken any confidential information from your company.

15

COMPUTER INSURANCE: RISKS AND PROTECTION

Insurance complements policies and internal controls. Coverage for the risks of business losses or liability exposure is a very important line of defense. However, insurance should never be seen as a substitute for other protective measures. The purpose of insurance is to indemnify the business owner/employer for loss of money, property, or other assets sustained through acts of nature, internal personnel, or outsiders. Acts insured against may include property loss or damage, vandalism, business interruption/economic loss, disaster-related costs, intellectual property infringement or loss, libel or slander, sexual harassment, invasion of privacy, unfair competition, embezzlement, forgery or alteration, extortion, computer systems fraud, or other fraudulent and dishonest acts. Insurance covers risks associated with computing and communications operations and systems. E-business is dependent on these technologies and needs insurance to cover, for example, computer and server downtime and various cyber crimes or torts.

TYPES OF COMPUTER INSURANCE POLICIES

There are a number of policies to cover the acts listed above. For computer equipment it is best to get separate property damage coverage rather than rely on a general business policy. Be sure to get replacement cost coverage, which pays to repair or replace damaged equipment at current prices. The policy should provide for the reproduction or replacement of lost data or media and electronic damage recovery.

Business interruption insurance will cover loss of sales or revenue due to a disaster, and, perhaps, computer crash losses, or losses related to Web operations and technology or e-commerce server downtime. Look for extra expense insurance for reimbursement of disaster-related costs over and above your normal operating expenses. Policies may also cover salaries, taxes, rent, and claims preparation costs. Besides general liability insurance, there are policies that provide commercial banks and other depository institutions with coverage for credit card fraud and computer-related crimes such as denial of service attacks and breaches of security committed by people outside the organization.

An insurance policy can be purchased in addition to a financial institution bond, which covers computer theft or fraud by employees. The policy expands that coverage to include third-party fraud and other technological exposures, such as losses from vandalism, computer viruses, computer hacking, software piracy, and "high-tech" extortion. The policy also covers fraud involving computer systems, computer programs, electronic money transfers, legal liability for service bureau operations, electronic communications to and from the institution, breaches of security for credit cards, and damage or destruction of programs and data. You may want your policy to also cover costs related to the legal liability of loss of computer capability or operational errors that produce inaccurate data or delayed processing for customers.

Specific website-related policies are becoming available to cover or augment general liability policies for intellectual property infringements and online defamation, slander, and libel. With e-business transacted on a worldwide basis, and the attendant risks and multiple legal jurisdictions, comprehensive international insurance policies should be considered. Internet-specific risk policies are emerging and should be examined.

Newer policies may cover financial losses from the theft of trade secrets. The secrets must be owned by the company and be in a recorded form.

EMPLOYMENT PRACTICES LIABILITY INSURANCE

Distributing standard antidiscrimination statements in employee handbooks is not enough to fend off claims. Education and sensitivity training are important, but in and of themselves cannot eliminate discrimination in the workplace. Prevention techniques like training and education, combined with the strategic use of employment practices liability (EPL) insurance, can provide a more effective program to reduce liabilities.

EMPLOYEE DISHONESTY INSURANCE

The purpose of employee dishonesty insurance is to indemnify an employer for loss of money or other property sustained through dishonest acts by employees. Acts insured against may include larceny, theft of money and securities, embezzlement, forgery or alteration, misappropriation, wrongful abstraction, willful misapplication, extortion, counterfeit currency, computer systems fraud, or other fraudulent and dishonest acts committed by the employee, whether acting alone or in collusion with others.

Property, real or personal—including money—is covered, whether owned by the employer or belonging to others. If an employee has access to funds or is authorized to buy, sell, ship, or store goods, he or she should be bonded in an amount adequate to offset potential thefts. It is logical to assume that the larger the firm's assets and the greater the turnover in volume of business, the more likely it is that a larger loss or series of losses may be concealed for a long period. If another party is involved, don't forget to look at their insurance for offsetting coverages or exclusions.

READING THE FINE PRINT

When evaluating any proposed insurance policy, look for required proof, notice, duty to defend, establishing damage or loss figures, specifically excepted or excluded perils,

171

proposed endorsements, and limits of liability. To counter coverage exclusions, define your "business activities" broadly.

Required Proof

A policy may require evidence of the actual problem, such as a disaster or a computer hacker, showing specific downtimes and losses of equipment. A proof of loss document must be signed and sworn to by the insured.

Some policies include a "manifest intent" clause, which can be used as proof when a particular result is certain to follow from an employee's conduct. However, there must be more than mistake, carelessness, or incompetence.

Notice

The notice provision is included in nearly every insurance policy. It is a potential pitfall in obtaining coverage for claims. Notice of a claim for recovery is required to be made to the insurance company within a reasonable time. Failure to satisfy this requirement can result in no indemnification for an otherwise covered claim.

The notice provision is usually included in the "conditions" section of a policy. Phrases such as "as soon as practicable" after an incident that could be eligible for a claim; "as soon thereafter" as the insured has knowledge of an incident; or "immediately" are used to describe when notice must be given.

Notice is often not given or is delayed because the insured is not sure of the proper insurance policy under which to make a claim, is ignorant of the policy coverage, lacks knowledge of the incident, or does not believe a claim will arise. Once the need to make a claim has been determined, it is best to inform the insurance company in writing as quickly as possible. In fact, even if the organization is unsure that its insurance will cover a claim, it is best to notify the insurance company of the possible claim, including information about the time, place, and circumstances of the loss.

Duty to Defend

Make sure the insurance company will defend an entire action if any part of the claim is within its insurance coverage. Some policies exclude the duty to defend certain actions.

Damages and the Rule of Certainty

Under this rule, a plaintiff must establish exact damages and valuations without recourse to speculation and conjecture and show a direct chain of causation running from the event to the loss sustained. The problem with computer-related damage claims is establishing the value of information. Make sure your policy includes provisions for establishing the value of information in computer-related claims.

RECOVERING FOR LOSSES

The following steps apply to making claims against insurance policies for losses.

❑ Consult with your attorney or insurance broker to identify the specific policy under which you can file a claim; clarify meanings of specific clauses relating to notice, subrogation (settlement) remedies, and proof of loss and the time frame for submitting the proof; identify what types of damages are excluded in your policy.

❑ Send notice of loss immediately to your broker or agent.

❑ Investigate the possible loss by using internal auditors, accountants, security and legal personnel, or an outside claims investigative agency specializing in computer-related damages or information loss; identifying and interviewing all staff with knowledge of the incident; identifying documents, electronic media, and other materials that might be relevant to determining loss or guilty parties; determining the extent of the loss and if any assets are retrievable.

❑ Terminate the employee(s) involved in an illegal act, but only on the advice of legal counsel and if your policy has a termination clause that excludes coverage if you retain a dishonest employee.

❑ Submit proof of loss to the insurance company.

❑ Cooperate with your insurance company; do not let the insurer charge that your company failed to cooperate with the investigation or in any other way. However, consult with your attorney about the nature and extent of your cooperation, especially about the confidentiality of documents.

❑ Do not settle with any party without discussing the settlement with your insurance company.

❑ Present accurate and provable/auditable losses in your claim.

❑ Be prepared to sue your insurance company if your claim is denied.

16

AUDIT
CHECKLISTS
AND MONITORING

LIABILITY EXPOSURE INVENTORY: CORPORATE CHECKLISTS

Use the following checklists to evaluate a company's exposure to liability for failing to comply with the *Federal Sentencing Guidelines for Organizations* or ethical and legal requirements.

Organizational Structure

Ask the following questions to identify structural problems:

❑ Are the business locations of the company widely dispersed, with key documents created at outlying locations and evidence of material transactions in more than one location?

❑ Is the company highly diversified, having numerous different businesses, each with its own accounting system?

❑ Is the company overly decentralized, with autonomous management?

❑ Does the organization have an organizational chart with management responsibilities clearly defined?

❑ Is management dominated by one or a few individuals?

❏ Does the company follow the practice of using different auditors for major segments?

❏ Does the company seem to need, but lack, an adequate internal audit staff?

❏ Do key financial positions, such as controller, not seem to stay filled for very long?

❏ Does the company have no outside general counsel, using special counsel for individual matters? Is outside general counsel changed frequently?

❏ Do the accounting and financial functions appear to be understaffed, resulting in constant crisis conditions?

❏ Does the audit closing require substantive adjusting of entries?

Ethical Environment

Evaluate the company's history with respect to:

❏ Labor-management relations

❏ Turnover of top executives

❏ Moonlighting and conflicts of interest by employees and executives

❏ Vandalism, theft, and sabotage by employees

❏ Corruption of customers

❏ Corruption by vendors or competitors

❏ Having a functioning compliance program

❏ Concern for truth in advertising or selling its products or services

❏ Convictions for business-related crimes

❏ Regulatory compliance

❏ Profitability

❏ Pending litigation and complaints against the firm by regulatory authorities, vendors, customers, creditors, and competitors

Codes of Ethics

Assess a company's specific code of ethics using the following questions:

❏ Does the ethics program emanate from the top of the organization:

    ❏ Board of Directors?

    ❏ audit or compliance committee?

    ❏ president/CEO?

    ❏ committee of senior managers?

❏ Is ethics known as a top-down program that everyone in the organization must comply with?

❏ Does the ethics officer hold a sufficiently influential position in the organization?

❏ Does the ethics officer have direct and unrestricted access to the Board, CEO, or other high-level officers?

❏ Does the ethics officer have a reputation of honesty and trust that is perceived by all officers, managers, and employees?

❏ Does the ethics officer have the support and resources to create, manage, and, if necessary, modify the ethics program?

❏ Does the ethics officer have the support of and liaison with legal, auditing, marketing, information systems, and other critical areas to carry out monitoring, investigation, and training activities?

❏ Is the ethics program periodically reinforced by top management?

❑ Does the organization have a written code of ethics? If yes,

  ❑ is the language used clear, understandable, and specific?

  ❑ has the code been distributed and communicated to all employees?

  ❑ does the code have the approval and signature of the organization's president?

❑ Does the organization seek to hire ethical, trustworthy employees?

❑ Does the organization provide employee training on ethics and decision making?

❑ Is there continual employee training on statutes, regulations, and specific liability exposures faced by the organization?

❑ Is there universal training on the organization's values and behavior covering all relevant laws affecting the organization, such as sexual harassment and discrimination?

❑ Have employees been told how their specific duties are affected by law and what to do about it?

❑ Is there a reporting mechanism, such as an ethics violation hotline (helpline or ombudsperson), and have its function and operations been explained to employees.?

❑ Is there an antiretaliation policy for those who report violations?

❑ Does management reinforce employees' belief that reporting violations can be done without fear of retribution?

❑ Have disciplinary procedures and possible sanctions for ethics violations been explained to all employees?

❑ Are employees trained on how to make a confidential report?

❏ Does the ethics code or the organization's policies restrict or prohibit

  ❏ outside employment?

  ❏ conflicts of interest?

  ❏ compromising or bribing customers?

  ❏ disclosure of trade secrets or proprietary information to unauthorized persons?

  ❏ fixing prices with competitors?

  ❏ gambling on the Internet while on the job?

  ❏ drug and alcohol abuse?

  ❏ stealing company property?

  ❏ using company property for a personal business?

  ❏ using company computer or communications systems for a personal business?

  ❏ destroying accounting records?

  ❏ destroying company property?

  ❏ falsifying time and attendance reports?

  ❏ falsifying production reports?

  ❏ falsifying expense reports?

  ❏ allowing unauthorized persons access to company property or proprietary information?

  ❏ disclosing information about customers, vendors, or third-party affiliates that has been designated private or confidential?

Industry, Company, and Management

Evaluate the company's overall position using the following questions:

❑ Does the industry of which the company is a part have a history of legal or regulatory violations?

❑ Has the company fallen on bad times, that is, is it losing money or market share; are its products or services becoming outdated?

❑ Does management's attitude toward audits and auditors exhibit hostility? Are auditors pressured to complete the audit quickly? Are auditors denied access to critical information, are information requests fulfilled unusually slowly, or are only copies of requested documents provided instead of originals? Do managers argue with auditors over the application of accounting principles that increase the earnings of the company?

❑ Is management overly concerned with short-term profit?

❑ Are financial decisions controlled by one person or a small, tight group?

❑ Does management have a healthy skepticism that all controls are working properly?

❑ Are internal controls few, weak, or loosely enforced?

❑ Does management state that internal controls and monitoring are part of management's responsibility in protecting the organization's assets?

❑ Is the company's management team experienced?

❑ Do policies and procedures describe levels of responsibilities and approvals?

❑ Is there an ongoing awareness of employee morale, employee attitudes, values, and job satisfaction?

❑ Are employees poorly supervised, abused, or placed under great stress to accomplish financial goals and objectives?

❑ Is there a solid awareness in the organization that failure to protect its assets could result in legal liability?

❑ Does the company have adequate, legally maintainable standards of recruitment and selection?

❏ Does the company have measures to screen applicants for sensitive positions before appointment, including

    ❏ employment verification?

    ❏ education verification?

    ❏ financial reliability?

    ❏ character?

❏ Are employees hired without due consideration for their honesty and integrity?

❏ Is there adequate orientation and training on security and privacy matters and company policies with respect to sanctions for violations?

❏ Does the management information system provide for:

    ❏ monitoring operational performance levels for (1) variations from plans and standards; (2) deviations from accepted or mandated policies, procedures, and practices; and (3) deviations from past quantitative relationships (ratios, proportions, percentages, trends, past performance levels, indices, etc.)?

    ❏ soliciting random feedback from or surveying customers, vendors, and suppliers for evidence of dissatisfaction, inefficiency, inconsistency with policies, corruption, or dishonesty by employees?

    ❏ studies of the people in the audit environment, responses to questions about their jobs, how they do them, and how they feel about them?

Employee Confidentiality Agreements

Ask the following questions about confidentiality agreements:

❑ Does the organization have a written and distributed policy on the use of confidential third-party information or records?

❑ Are employees required to read and sign a confidentiality agreement regarding information privacy?

❑ Are sensitive/vital software and documentation secure?

COMPUTER SECURITY AUDIT

Computer protection managers are responsible for

- advising personnel of the importance of computer security when creating notes or reports, stressing both the privacy and confidentiality aspects;

- advising personnel of the proper way to store computer media; and

- consulting with records storage staff about the organization's document management policies.

The following lists cover security of computer facilities, network access and operations control, websites, records, and off-site storage.

Facility Security Checklist

❑ Does the company have an access control and physical security system?

❑ Is the system totally functional?

❑ Are there security guards at the computer site?

❑ Are all packages and briefcases searched going in and out?

❑ Are storage media disks marked with a company logo or other identifiers?

❑ Are company storage media leaving the facility subject to search and examination, including contents?

❑ Does the company require positive ID for all personnel entering the facility, data center, or computer room?

❑ Are visitors controlled?

❑ Is there a security log for visitors and employees to sign?

❑ Is access to the data center limited to working hours or office shift hours?

❑ Is video surveillance used?

Data Processing Areas/Rooms/Equipment Checklist

❑ During what hours do the computer areas operate?

❑ Are employees who are authorized to enter data processing areas required to use a company-issued personal identification device?

❑ Is positive ID required for all vendors or consultants entering the computer or communications areas?

❑ Are all other employees prohibited from freely entering computer areas?

❑ Are signs posted on all entry doors prohibiting all unauthorized persons from entering?

❑ Are guards or data processing supervisors positioned to observe any unauthorized entry?

❑ Under what conditions, if any, are unauthorized persons given access to data processing areas?

❑ Are they then under constant observation?

❑ Is an access log kept of all persons who enter the data processing area?

❏ Are internal fire prevention inspections conducted regularly?

❏ Is the fire suppression system for the computer room tested regularly?

❏ Does the computer center have fire retardant walls?

❏ Is the computer room located under a large water system, the company cafeteria, or bathrooms?

❏ Do computers have an uninterruptible power supply and surge protection equipment?

❏ Does the company have an access control and physical security system?

❏ Is the system totally functional?

❏ Are personal computers, lap- and palmtops, and notebooks secured with an alarm system, lock-down bars, cables, chains, fasteners, or other physical security devices?

❏ Are disk drives secured with key locks?

Computer/Network Access and Operations Controls Checklist

❏ Are standard logon procedures enforced through identification/verification defenses?

❏ Does someone have administrative responsibility for access authorization?

❏ Is only built-in user authentication utilities software used for secure access?

❏ Are system-stored passwords and codes encrypted?

❏ Is the sharing and disclosure of passwords allowed?

❏ Are there written policy and procedures on selecting and disclosing passwords?

COMPUTER SECURITY AUDIT

❏ Are passwords kept secret and known only to their users?

❏ Are passwords prohibited from being displayed near or on the user's computer?

❏ Are chosen passwords difficult to guess and easy to remember, having a minimum length and both alpha and numeric characters?

❏ Are system-assigned/generated passwords mandated?

❏ Are passwords changed regularly (monthly, every 60 days or three months if user-selected; six months for system-generated passwords, but no longer than once a year for any password)?

❏ Are passwords and other access codes deactivated immediately when an employee leaves the company?

❏ Are periodic audits performed to determine if the company's password security policies and procedures are being followed and are still effective?

❏ Are all accesses logged?

❏ Are the date/time and location of access logged?

❏ Is establishment of authorizations by levels of authority or levels of security?

❏ Is third-party access authorization software used?

❏ Are there exceptions to detection logging systems?

❏ Does the operator have restricted access to all programs and data files in the mainframe?

❏ Are critical or sensitive data files protected from unauthorized access with masking techniques or intruder alarms?

❏ Are critical or sensitive data files protected from unauthorized update with tampering or change-detection techniques?

❏ Are employees allowed to load unauthorized software onto the company's computers?

❏ Is virus-checking software installed on all computers in the organization?

❏ Are there periodic audits of employee computers for unlicensed software?

❏ Are there any operating or processing controls (change and file controllers) that can detect fraudulent manipulation of data?

❏ Does the operator maintain a record of what jobs are processed?

❏ Are daily transactions summarized?

❏ Are exception reports generated?

❏ Is there a transaction log?

❏ Is the system easily modified?

❏ Are there restrictions on who has access to production copies of live data or programs?

❏ Is the computer/communications network protected by firewalls, intrusion detection, or other technology to control access?

❏ Are dial-up lines monitored and recorded for repeated failed access attempts?

❏ Are there vulnerability scanning, security activity reporting, and penetration analysis capabilities in the computer security program?

❏ Are standard mainframe access control measures employed once dial-up connection has been made?

❏ Does the network or data communications system use encryption with key management, public key infrastructure, digital certificates, virtual public networks, or other authentication, security, and audit measures?

SECURING A WEBSITE

Website security includes restricting access to the internal Web server and to a mainframe, an intranet, the Internet, or the World Wide Web. Another area of security concern is transactions between the company's website and suppliers or customers. Internal security requires access controls and firewalls. A *firewall* is a configuration of security access control, filtering, and screening technology designed to keep unauthorized traffic out of an unsecured and untrusted network. Communications and transaction security often require the use of encryption and digital signature technologies.

Checklist

When evaluating website security, ask the following questions:

❑ Has company policy defined the authorized traffic and access into and from the website?

❑ Is the security of Internet connections adequate?

❑ Is there access control technology or a complete firewall system for the Web server and other computing and communications equipment with online connections?

❑ Does the communications/transaction system have the ability to authenticate customer and client information?

❑ Are credit card transactions protected by the secure sockets layer (SSL) encryption protocol or another secure payments method?

❑ Does the website provider have a comprehensive security policy that is communicated to its employees? Is this policy enforced?

❑ Are the employees trained to be competent in security procedures and technology?

❑ Are all security measures monitored and audited?

❏ What will the Internet or website provider do if service is interrupted?

BACKUP CHECKLIST

Secure backup is a necessity to prevent possible loss of data. Evaluate the security of a company's backup using the following questions:

❏ Are backup files kept at a secondary site? If yes, are there any controls?

❏ Do data backup and records retention and maintenance follow either legal requirements or company policy?

❏ Are all serial numbers and software license information recorded and kept in a secure location?

❏ Is sensitive/vital software and documentation secure (payroll records, personnel records, accounts receivable information, etc.)?

❏ Are there records that, if destroyed, would seriously impair the company's ability to resume operations quickly? If so, is a backup file kept at a secondary site, and are there any controls?

DISASTER RECOVERY CHECKLIST

It is necessary to be prepared for a loss of computer data as a result of a disaster (e.g., fire, flood, earthquake). Use the following questions to evaluate a company's disaster preparedness:

❏ Does management recognize the following essential procedures of a disaster plan?

  ❏ identification of critical information

  ❏ recovery of critical information

- ❏ designation of alternate sites
- ❏ plan testing and evaluation

❏ Is there a thorough, appropriate, and tested disaster recovery plan?

❏ Are restart procedures fully documented?

❏ Are the resources shared by another company?

CREATING TRUSTWORTHY RECORDS

For records to be reliable, the records system, whether physical or electronic, must capture each record's

- content—what is in the record;
- structure—the mechanism, machine, hardware, and software used to create the record;
- context—the business or legal activity for which the record was created and its purpose; and
- retrieval—for its life cycle, particularly for the length of time required by law.

The process or system producing records must be shown to be reliable and accurate, providing proof that a record was produced

- as part of a regularly conducted business activity, at regular times, or as a regular activity but at times that were irregular;
- by methods that ensure accuracy, or where accuracy could be demonstrated via audits, regular monitoring, or quality control;
- with timeliness, that is, simultaneously or within a short time after the activity; and
- by system procedures that accurately reveal the steps in creating, modifying, duplicating, retention, and destruction.

All procedures, controls, monitoring, audits, and training programs associated with records management should be documented.

EVALUATING OFF-SITE STORAGE FACILITIES

Off-site storage facilities offer a variety of sites, protection, and services. When selecting a facility, a company must first know its requirements for records retention, which should include

- the amount of storage space needed;

- how records must be cataloged;

- how often records will be sent or brought to the facility; and

- how records must be stored.

Once the company's requirements are known, evaluate the facility regarding location and security.

Location

Generally, an off-site facility should be far enough away from the company that it won't experience the same disaster, yet close enough to retrieve important records quickly. Find out if the storage facility is open to its clients 24 hours per day, 365 days a year.

Security

There are obviously different levels of security. Security for an off-site storage facility can be evaluated by site, access control, intrusion detection, fire suppression, environmental controls, storage, media control, retrieval and transport, and records management.

- **Site security** can consist of fencing, perimeter lighting, closed circuit television, outdoor intrusion detection, and guards at gates.

- **Access control** makes it possible to identify with as much certainty as possible any person seeking entrance to the facility.

  ❏ What access control system does the facility use?

  ❏ Does the system log all attempts by individuals seeking access?

  ❏ How fast can access privileges be changed?

  ❏ How fast can new cards be issued?

- **Intrusion detection**

  ❏ Is the interior of the storage facility protected by an intrusion detection system and closed circuit television that is monitored?

  ❏ How is the system monitored?

  ❏ Is the system monitored 24 hours per day, 7 days per week?

  ❏ Is the intrusion detection system wired directly to the police department?

  ❏ If the system is in-house and proprietary, what is the guard response force?

  ❏ If the system is tied into a central station service, whose is it, and what is their U.L. rating? Is the central station operated 24 hours per day?

- **Fire detection and suppression**

  ❏ What type of fire detectors and fire suppression system are installed?

  ❏ Who monitors the system, and is it done 24 hours per day?

  ❏ Is the fire detection system wired to the fire department?

- **Environmental controls**

  ❑ What equipment provides for temperature, humidity, air conditioning, dust control, and water or humidity detection?

- **Storage**

  ❑ Are the vaults, safes, or storage files rated for burglary, fire, or media?

- **Media control**

  ❑ Is there periodic inventory of stored media? (A unit of media is controlled individually.)

  ❑ Is there an effective media maintenance program?

- **Retrieval and transport**

  ❑ Is there 24 hours per day accessibility, 7 days per week and 24 hours per day courier service, 7 days per week?

  ❑ Are transport vehicles environmentally controlled, equipped with intrusion detection and alarms, and equipped with a fire suppression system?

  ❑ What is the maximum response time?

- **Records management** A facility should offer services designed to make the task of records management easier. Inventory of records, retention periods, removal authorizations, and maintaining record pick-up schedules are basic services. Some facilities offer copying of optical and magnetic media and have shredders, pulpers, and disintegrators for destroying obsolete records or degaussing for erasing magnetic media.

  ❑ Does the facility offer clients online access to the complete inventory of their records?

  ❑ Does facility software integrate with the client's in-house document management program?

  ❑ Are clients given an affidavit certifying the destruction of records?

GLOSSARY

Access.   To instruct, communicate with, store in, or retrieve data from a computer system or network.

Access control.   Means of restricting entry/access to a computer room, terminal, or network.

Automated Clearing House (ACH).   Facilities for computer processing of large-volume financial transactions and transferring, via electronic communication channels, information of such transactions to member banks, bank customers, and others.

Alteration.   Any material change of the terms of a writing fraudulently made by a party thereto.

Audit.   A process of examining administrative or computer procedures or controls to determine their reliability.

Authentic.   Of undisputed origin or authorship; reliable; genuine; credible; authoritative and original (as document).

Authentication.   The process of proving that someone or something, such as a message or a transaction, is genuine or valid; in a computer system, identifying a user.

Authorization.   A right, granted by management, to approve.

Beneficiary.   In funds transfers, the person to be paid by the beneficiary's bank.

Biometrics (in security systems).   The machine/computer identification and verification of persons based on biological or physiological measurements. In general operation, the system consists of a device that scans or replicates the characteristic to be measured. That is, the device may record a series of words; photograph or laser scan a fingerprint or an eye's vessel pattern; or measure the length of a person's fingers and the spread of the hand, the speed, pressure, and size of a person's signature, or the speed and rhythm of keystrokes in data entry. A computer and appropriate software store, process, and analyze the measurements.

Checksum. A short string of data that represents the content of an electronic document.

Clickwrap. An action used in a Web-posted privacy policy for the consumer to agree to the terms of the policy. A couple of clicks mean "I agree" via a click/statement. A "clickwrap" is the same as a "shrinkwrap" license/contract.

Collective or aggregate knowledge. Knowledge possessed by several employees that adds up to willful knowledge or yields a guilty state of mind, as required by the statute. The employing organization can be liable for violating a law.

Complicity rule. The rule that an accomplice is liable for assisting, encouraging, or failing to prevent a crime.

Computer network. A set of related, remotely connected devices and communication facilities including more than one computer system; the interconnection of electronic communication with a computer through remote terminals; a complex consisting of two or more interconnected computers.

Computer system. A set of related, connected or unconnected computer equipment, devices, or computer programs and data that performs functions including, but not limited to, logic, arithmetic, data storage and retrieval of communication, and control.

Condoned an offense. Knew of an offense and did not take reasonable steps to prevent or terminate the offense.

Confidentiality. Ensuring that information is not made available or disclosed to unauthorized individuals. Electronic messages may be encrypted to ensure confidentiality.

Consequential damages. Damages awarded for errors made. The Uniform Commercial Code, Article 4A, limits the amount of damages businesses may recover from banks that commit errors. Unless there is an express agreement, banks cannot be held liable for consequential damages for errors made in connection with funds transfers.

Contract. An agreement between two or more parties that creates an obligation to do or not to do a particular thing. Three fundamental legal requirements of commercial contracts are an offer, acceptance, and consideration or payment.

Control activities. The policies and procedures that help ensure management directives are carried out. They include a range of activities as diverse as approvals, authorizations, verifications, reconciliations, reviews of operating performance, security of assets, and segregation of duties.

Control environment. The integrity, ethical values, and competence of an entity's people; management's philosophy and operating style; the way management assigns authority and responsibility and organizes and develops its people; the attention and direction provided by the board of directors.

Cookies. One of the main, once surreptitious, methods of gathering information about website visitors. A "cookie" allows information to be read off or written to a computer's hard drive, such as which websites a person visited and what action was taken at those sites. Cookies are a way for website providers to obtain and store information about their users and to use that information for various marketing purposes. Because users often do not know about this method of information gathering, privacy issues may be raised.

Credit transfer. A funds transfer in which the instruction is given by the person making the payment. U.C.C. Article 4A governs these transfers.

Damages. Compensation awarded for actual loss or injury to the victim. *Punitive damages* are awarded over and above a loss or injury and vary with the degree of punishment imposed.

Data manipulation. The altering of data before or during the input process.

Digital signature. An authentication method for computer messages.

Distributed database system. A computer system with the database distributed over several sites.

Documentation. All records on how a computer system was designed and how it operates.

Due care. The degree of care that a reasonable person would exercise to prevent harm that was reasonably foreseeable in the event that such care were not taken.

Due diligence. "Such a measure of prudence, activity, or assiduity, as is properly to be expected from, and ordinarily exercised by, a reasonable and prudent man under the particular circumstances; not measured by any absolute standard, but depending on the relative facts of the special case" *(Black's Law Dictionary).*

Electronic Funds Transfer Act (EFTA). The federal statute that covers a wide range of electronic funds transfers, including point-of-sale transactions and other consumer payments. If any portion of a funds transfer is covered by EFTA, the whole funds transfer is excluded from U.C.C. Article 4A.

Electronic record. A record created, generated, sent, communicated, received, or stored by electronic means. A record is "information that is inscribed on a tangible medium or that is stored in an electronic or other medium and is retrievable in perceivable form."

Electronic signature. An electronic sound, symbol, or process attached to or logically associated with a record and executed or adopted by a person with the intent to sign the record.

Evidence. Information presented in court to the trier of fact as proof of the facts in dispute or in support of the theory of a party. Evidentiary forms are real, testimonial, documentary, and demonstrative.

Extortion. Coercion to obtain property by inducing fear, using threats of or actual force or violence.

False acceptance. In an access control system, the admission of an imposter or an unauthorized user. Also referred to as false positive.

False rejection. In an access control system, the false rejection of authorized personnel. Also referred to as false negative.

Fedwire. The Federal Reserve wire transfer network. Wire transfers made by Fedwire are governed by Federal Reserve Regulation J (12 *CFR* Part 210).

Fines. Monetary punishment imposed for an infraction. Under the FSGO, fines are usually based on an analysis first; a base fine, which is a measure of the seriousness of the offense; and a culpability score, which is a measure of how culpable the organization was in committing and responding to the offense.

Flagrant organizational indifference. The conscious avoidance by an organization of learning about and observing the requirements of a statute.

Forgery. The fraudulent making or altering of an instrument that apparently creates or alters a legal liability of another.

Foreseeability. The legal obligation of one party to protect another party against foreseeable, intentional wrongs done by a third party. "The probability of injury by one to the legally protected interests of another is the basis for the law's creation of a duty to avoid such injury, and foresight of harm lies at the foundation of the duty to use care and therefore of negligence. The broad test of negligence is what a reasonably prudent person would foresee and would do in the light of this foresight under the circumstances" (*American Jurisprudence* 2d, Sect. 135).

Hash total. A sum formed for control purposes by adding fields that are not normally related by a unit of measure. This is a verification method using a total compiled from numbers such as part numbers, invoice numbers, or customer account numbers.

Identification. A process that enables recognition of a user by a computer system; passwords and biometric systems are two methods of access control/identification.

Integrity. An unbroken state; completeness; original perfect condition. It applies to the content of a message and whether it has been altered. Message authentication techniques may be used to ensure the integrity of electronic messages.

Integrity programs. Compliance programs that are more amorphous, yet more broadly based, than traditional compliance programs, which are essentially specific law-based. Integrity programs are more concerned with ethical behavior throughout the organization and relations with outside stakeholders.

Intentionally. Purposely; desiring to cause consequences.

Intermediary bank. A receiving bank other than the originator's bank or the beneficiary's bank.

Intimidation. Unlawful coercion; duress; putting in fear (of harm). The state must arise from the willful conduct of the accused.

Knowingly. Acting with awareness of the nature of one's conduct; having actual knowledge of or acting with deliberate ignorance of or reckless disregard for specific legal prohibitions.

Liability, derivative. Responsibility for acts and intent of corporate officers and agents that is imputable to the corporate entity.

Liability of directors and officers. Responsibility for failing to perform a statutory or a common law duty or use ordinary care and prudence. Special liabilities have been imposed by the Securities Act of 1933 and 1934 and the Foreign Corrupt Practices Act. Liability may also arise from directors' inadequate attention to overseeing and monitoring of an organization's compliance systems.

Liability, strict. Responsibility for the act only; requires no proof of intent to commit the act.

Liability, vicarious. Responsibility for the actionable conduct of employees performed in the scope of their employment. This traditional doctrine applies to aiding and abetting a crime or a conspiracy to commit a crime or actions taken with the knowledge and intention of facilitating the commission of a crime.

Logic bomb. A computer program residing in a computer that is executed at appropriate or periodic times to determine conditions or states of a computer system and that facilitates the perpetration of an unauthorized act.

Monitoring. Examining, inspecting, observing, scrutinizing, or checking systematically. The monitoring process assesses the quality of an internal control system's performance over time. Monitoring, like quality checks, should be a routine business practice.

Motivation. The deeply felt understanding of the dangers, both direct and collateral, of prosecution and conviction. It is a key element leading to the establishment of a compliance program.

Mouse type. Tiny type (5 point or smaller) used on websites to obfuscate and defeat any attempt at reading and understanding a privacy policy.

Negligence. A tort involving the duty to use reasonable care. It is designed to protect persons from unintentional harm from the conduct of others. Criteria for determining negligence are vague.

Nonrepudiation. Inability to disclaim, renounce, or reject (as when an electronic message is believed to be authentic).

Notice. Statement of specific knowledge of the existence of a fact or condition. Notice may give rise to a duty to protect, or at least to investigate a situation.

"Ostrich" instruction. A legal instruction that permits a jury to infer guilty knowledge from a combination of suspicion and indifference to the truth (see *U.S. v. Giovannetti*).

Parity. A method of verifying the integrity of transmitted data by checking the odd-even relationship of the bits.

Password. A protected word or string of characters that identifies a user, a specific resource, or an access type.

Payment order. An instruction by a business, or the originator of a funds transfer, to its bank to pay or credit an intended recipient a specific amount.

Privacy. The right to keep something from public view or knowledge. The right to privacy belongs to or is the property of a particular individual or group of persons.

Promulgate. To publish, announce.

Prove. To meet the burden of establishing the fact, the burden of persuading the triers of fact that the existence of the fact is more probable than its non-existence. Proof is the conclusion drawn from the evidence about the existence of particular facts.

Prudent. Circumspect in action or in determining any line of conduct.

Public Key Infrastructure (PKI). A digital certificate system of validated private and public encryption key pairs involved in an Internet transaction. A PKI system consists of key management capabilities from signing, verification, encryption/decryption, revocation, and directories of certificates, along with means for key backup and recovery.

Questioned document. A communication that has been disputed in whole or in part in respect to its authenticity, identity, or origin.

Reasonable. "Fit and appropriate to the end in view" (*Black's Law Dictionary*).

Reckless. Careless, heedlessly indifferent to consequences; showing lack of due caution.

Recoverability. A control objective of contingency plans, data/information backup, and retention to minimize downtime and ensure operational recovery of information and communications systems.

Reliability. The property of meeting management control objectives of accuracy, completeness, timeliness, security, auditability, and recoverability. Information systems may have to meet a definition of reliability based on a set of control objectives.

Responsible corporate officer doctrine. A tenet that applies to any corporate officer or employee "standing in responsible relation" to an act forbidden. Liability can arise if the officer could have prevented or corrected a violation and failed to do so.

This is a critical doctrine with significant implications. An officer has a positive duty to *seek out and remedy violations when they occur*; and a duty to implement measures that will *ensure that violations will not occur.* The responsible corporate officer doctrine derives from the

Food, Drug and Cosmetic Act (see *U.S. v. Park*) and the Clean Water Act. Although normally applied to services and products that affect the health and well-being of the public, the doctrine could easily cover mental well-being, such as privacy. The doctrine forces corporate officers to define which risks they should know of, because they are likely to be held to an affirmative duty of care concerning those risks.

Risk. The chance of loss; exposure to a peril, in most cases measurable by probability. A pure risk applies only to the possibility of loss.

Risk analysis. The identification of risk factors, followed by measurement or quantification to determine possible loss frequency or severity. Statistical models, such as probability analysis, Bayesian theory, or Poisson distributions, may be used to predict future losses.

Risk assessment. The identification and analysis of relevant risks to achievement of control objectives, forming a basis for determining how risks should be managed.

Risk control. The identification, analysis, measurement, and elimination, reduction, or avoidance of risk.

Risk exposure survey. An inventory of loss exposure possibilities. This is an ongoing process with emphasis on evaluation, experience, and judgment.

Risk management. The encompassing process of risk exposure identification, the judgmental or technical analysis of risk, and the control or elimination of risk.

Rogue employees. Workers who, for their own benefit, commit illegal acts, or whose conduct violates company policy and procedure despite in-place efforts to prevent such acts.

Scienter. Knowledge, referring to those wrongs or crimes requiring a knowledge of wrong in order to constitute the offense.

Sender. The customer in whose name a payment order is issued (if the order is the authorized order of the customer under U.C.C. 4A-203 subsection (a), or is effective as the order of the customer under U.C.C. 4A-203 subsection (b)).

Signature. The traditional manner of making a document, such as a contract, legally effective. A signing may be a symbol with present intention to authenticate a writing.

Simulation and modeling. The creation of a system to duplicate one already in existence.

Source document. A form for recording data, usually the first record.

Spoliation. The act of destroying a document or of injuring or tampering with it so as to destroy its value as evidence. Spoliation is punished as an obstruction of justice offense.

Substantial authority personnel. Individuals who, within the scope of their authority, exercise a substantial measure of discretion in acting on behalf of an organization. The term includes high-level personnel, individuals who exercise substantial supervisory authority, and any other individuals who, although not part of an organization's management, nevertheless exercise substantial discretion when acting within the scope of their authority.

Tampering. The unauthorized modification of a computer device or system that causes its degradation or malfunction.

Timeliness. A control objective of avoiding disruption or delays in data processing or transmission.

Tort. An injury or wrong arising from a breach of duty created by law.

Transaction log. A printout delineating all interactive input, process, and outputs on any file.

Trojan horse. Computer instructions secretly inserted in a computer program so that when it is executed in a computer, unauthorized acts are performed.

Value-added network (VAN). A private, secure network and other services for EDI (electronic data interchange).

Verification. Checking for accuracy; confirming correctness and authenticity by sworn or equivalent confirmation or truth.

Virtual Private Network (VPN). A collection of technologies that creates site-to-site secure connections or "tunnels" over regular Internet lines.

Virus. A self-propagating Trojan horse.

Wholesale wire transfers. Transfer payments principally between businesses or financial institutions.

Willful blindness or indifference. Intentional avoidance of knowing that a situation or act will incriminate. Willfulness is a disregard for the governing statute and an indifference to its requirements.

Willfully ignorant of the offense. Intentionally unaware of an infraction. If an individual did not investigate the possible occurrence of unlawful conduct despite knowledge of circumstances that would lead a reasonable person to investigate whether unlawful conduct had occurred, that person was willfully ignorant.

Wiretapping. Interception of data communications signals with the intent to gain access to data transmitted over communications circuits.

Wrongful act. "Any act which in the ordinary course (of business) will infringe upon the rights of another to his damage" (*Black's Law Dictionary*).

SELECTED REFERENCES

Baker, D. and Brandel, R. *Law of Electronic Funds Transfer Systems*. New York: Warren, Gorham & Lamont, 1988.

Beniger, J. *The Control Revolution*. Cambridge, MA: Harvard University Press, 1986.

Bing, G. *Due Diligence Techniques and Analysis*. Westport, CT: Quorm Books, 1996.

Bologna, Jack and Shaw, Paul. *Fraud Awareness Manual*. Madison, WI: Assets Protection, 1995.

Brickey, Kathleen. *Corporate Criminal Liability*. Deerfield, IL: Callaghan & Co., 1989.

Brinson, Dianne J. and Radcliffe, Mark F. *Multimedia Law and Business Handbook*. Menlo Park, CA: Ladera Press, 1996.

A Business Checklist for Direct Marketers. The Direct Marketing Association, 1111 19th St., N.W., Suite 1100, Washington, DC 20036-3603, (202) 955-5030.

Business Conference Board. *Corporate Ethics*. New York: The Conference Board, 1990.

Cate, F. *Privacy in the Information Age*. New York: Brookings Institution Press, 1998.

Coase, R.H. *The Firm, the Market and the Law*. Chicago: University of Chicago Press, 1988.

Committee of Sponsoring Organizations of the Treadway Commission (COSO). *Internal Control—Integrated Framework*. New York: The Committee of Sponsoring Organizations of the Treadway Commission, 1992.

Disaster Recovery Yellow Pages. Newton, MA: The Systems Audit Group, 2000.

Dorr, Robert C. and Munch, Christopher H. *Protecting Trade Secrets, Patents, Copyrights, and Trademarks*. 2nd ed. New York: John Wiley & Sons, Inc., 1995.

Electronic Privacy Information Center. *Cryptography and Liberty 2000—An International Survey of Encryption Policy*. Washington, DC: Electronic Privacy Information Center, 2000.

Etzioni, A. *Limits of Privacy*. New York: Basic Books, 1999.

SELECTED REFERENCES

Ezor, J. *Clicking Through*. New York: Bloomberg Press, 2000.

Fischer, L. Richard. *The Law of Financial Privacy*. 2nd ed. New York: Warren, Gorham & Lamont, 1991.

Fombrun, C. *Reputation*. Cambridge, MA: Harvard Business School Press, 1996.

Fukuyama, F. *Trust*. New York: The Free Press, 1995.

Global Cyberspace Jurisdiction Project. *Achieving Legal and Business Order in Cyberspace: A Report on Global Jurisdiction Issues Created by the Internet*. Chicago: American Bar Association, 2000.

Goldblatt, M. *Preventive Law in Corporate Practice*. New York: Matthew Bender, 1991.

Gonclaves, M. *Firewalls: A Complete Guide*. New York: McGraw-Hill, 2000.

Hagel, J. *Shaping Markets When Customers Make the Rules*. Cambridge, MA: Harvard Business School Press, 1999.

Hannon, L. *Legal Side of Private Security*. Westport, CT: Greenwood Publishing Group, 1992.

Hartsfield, H. *Investigating Employee Conduct*. Deerfield, IL: Callaghan & Co., 1988.

Keeton, W. *Prosser and Keeton on Torts*. St. Paul, MN: West Publishing Co., 1984.

Kramer, M.W. *Investigative Techniques in Complex Financial Crimes*. Washington, DC: National Institute on Economic Crime, 1989.

Kraus, M. and Tipton, H.F., eds. *Information Security Handbook*. 2nd ed. New York: Auerbach Publications, 1999.

Lee, Lewis C. and Davidson, J. Scott. *Intellectual Property for the Internet*. New York: John Wiley & Sons, Inc., 1997.

Lessing, L. *Code and Other Laws of Cyberspace*. New York: Basic Books, 1999.

Milgrim, Roger M. *Milgrim on Trade Secrets*. Albany, NY: Matthew Bender, 1994.

Nichols, R. *Defending Your Digital Assets*. New York: McGraw-Hill, 2000.

Nimmer, Raymond T. *The Law of Computer Technology*. Rev. ed. New York: Warren, Gorham & Lamont, 1994.

Parker, Donn B. *Fighting Computer Crime*. New York: John Wiley & Sons, Inc., 1998.

Perritt, Henry H., Jr. *Law and the Information Superhighway*. New York: John Wiley & Sons, Inc., 1996.

Privacy Journal. Compilation of State and Federal Privacy Laws. Providence, RI.

SELECTED REFERENCES

Regan, P. *Legislating Privacy.* Chapel Hill: University of North Carolina Press, 1996.

Reichheld, F. *The Loyalty Effect.* Cambridge, MA: Harvard Business School Press, 1996.

Renesse, Rudolf Van. *Optical Document Security.* New York: John Wiley & Sons, Inc., 1995.

Shaw, Paul. *Managing Legal and Security Risks in Computing and Communications.* Woburn, MA: Butterworth Heinemann, 1998.

Shaw, Paul and Bologna, Jack. *Avoiding Cyber Fraud in Small Businesses.* New York: John Wiley & Sons, 2000.

Skupsky, D. *Legal Requirements for Microfilm, Computer, and Optical Disk Records.* Denver: Information Requirements Clearinghouse, 1994.

Sigler, J. and Murphy, J. *Corporate Lawbreaking and Interactive Compliance.* Westport, CT: Greenwood Publishing Group, 1991.

Vergani, James V. and Shue, Virginia V. *Fundamentals of Computer-High Technology Law.* Philadelphia: American Law Institute/American Bar Association, 1991.

Villa, J. *Banking Crimes: Fraud, Money Laundering, and Embezzlement.* New York: Clark Boardman, 1988.

Warren, Samuel D. and Brandeis, Louis D. "The Right to Privacy." *Harvard Law Review* 4 (1890): 193.

Wasik, M. *Crime and the Computer.* Cary, NC: Oxford University Press, 1991.

Wheildon, C. *Type & Layout.* Berkeley, CA: Strathmore Press, 1995.

Wood, Charles W. *Information Security Policies Made Easy.* Sausalito, CA: Baseline Software, 1994.

Wright, Benjamin. *The Law of Electronic Commerce: EDI, E-mail, and Internet.* 2nd ed. Boston: Little, Brown & Company, 1995.

SELECTED
WEBSITES

Marketing

Council for Internet Commerce, www.commercestandard.com

Internet Advertising Bureau, http://www.iab.net/advertise/metricsource.html

Privacy

AICPA/CICA SysTrust Principles and Criteria for Systems Reliability, http://www.aicpa.org

American Society for Testing and Materials, Committees E31.17 and E31.20, http://www.astm.org

British Standard 7799 Code of Practice for Information Security Management and Specification for Information Security Management Systems, http://www.bsi.org.uk/disc/

Computer-Based Patient Record Institute, *Guidelines for Data Security,* http://www.cpri.org

Electronic Privacy Information Center, http://www.epic.org

Information Systems, Audit, and Control Foundation, *COBIT—Governance, Control, and Audit Objectives for Information and Related Technology,* http://www.isaca.org/cobit.htm

International Federation of Accountants, *Managing Security of Information,* http://www.ifac.org/StandardsAndGuidance/InformationTechnology.html

International Information Security Foundation, *Generally Accepted Systems Security Principles,* http://web.mit.edu/security/www/gassp1.html

National Institute of Standards, Computer Security Resource Clearinghouse, http://csrc.nist.gov

Organization for Economic Development, Paris, *Guidelines for the Security of Information Systems*, http://www.oecd.org//dsti/sti/it/secur/prod/esecur.htm

Information Security and Intellectual Property

CERT Coordination Center, Carnegie Mellon Engineering Institute, www.cert.org

Cornell University, *U.S. Code*, http://www.law.cornell.edu/uscode/17/

Franklin Pierce Law Center, http://www.fplc.edu/tfield/order.htm

ILTweb Institute for Learning Technologies, http://www.ilt.columbia.edu/projects/copyright/index.html

Index to Patent Classification, http://sunsite.unc.edu/patents/index.html

Manual of Patent Classification, http://sunsite.unc.edu/patents/intropat.html#manual

Master-McNeil Trademark Resources, http://www.naming.com/naming/trademark.html

National Information Infrastructure, http://iitf.doc.gov

Network Solutions Internet domain names registrations, http://rs.internic.net/domain-info/internic-domain-6.html

University of Arkansas, *Copyright and Intellectual Property*, http://www.uark.edu/depts/comminfo/www/copyright.html

U.S. Copyright Office, http://lcweb.loc.gov/copyright/

U.S. Patent and Trademark Office, http://www.uspto.gov

U.S. Patent Database, http://patents.cnidr.org:4242

U.S. Trademark Act (full text), http://www.law.cornell.edu/lanham/lanham.table.html

INDEX

access, 195
access control(s), 129, 132, 195
  computers,
      systems/networks, 130
  false acceptance, 131
  false rejection, 131
  identity verification, 131
affiliate, 52
Age Discrimination in
     Employment Act, 24
alteration, 195
American Institute of Certified
     Public Accountants, 87
American Law Institute, 76
Americans with Disabilities Act,
     38
applications programming
     interface (API), 126, 133
assets
  intangible, 145
  protection of, 89
audit
  assertions, 90
  attestations, 90
  compliance, 89
  detecting and preventing
     function, 91
  financial, 89
  trail, 125
auditing checklists
  codes of ethics, 179
  computer security, 184-188
  corporate liability exposures,
     177-183

disaster recovery, 190
  employee confidentiality
     agreements, 183-184
  ethical environment, 178
  facility security, 184-186
  file/data backups, 92, 190
  offsite storage, 192-194
  trustworthy records, 191-192
  website operator's privacy
     assessment, 17
  website security, 189-190
auditors, 80
authentication, 126, 138, 195
authentication/verification
     systems, 126-129, 138
authorization, 89, 195
Automated Clearing House
     (ACH), 195

backups, 92
Bank Holding Company Act,
     49
beneficiary, 195
biometric(s), 125, 195
  evaluation and selection
     criteria, 130-132
  "layering" biometrics, 129
  privacy concerns, 130-131
  techniques, products,
     systems, and vendors,
     126-128, 133
Brandeis, Louis D., 21
bribery, 151
browsers, 14

Cable Act, 25
Cable Communications Policy
    Act, 25
Caremark International, Inc.,
    75
  compliance program, 75
certificate authorities, 142
  function of, 142
  management, 142
  privacy, 142
  trust, 142
checksum, 196
Children's Online Privacy
    Protection Act (COPPA),
    59-63
  liability risk audit checklist,
    61-63
  privacy objectives, 51-61
  privacy requirements for
    websites, 60-61
Clean Water Act, 78
clickwrap, 196
Code of Fair Information
    Practices, 23
codes of conduct, 76, 104
collective knowledge, 195
commercial information, 145
Committee of Sponsoring
    Organizations (COSO), 87
Communications Assistance
    for Law Enforcement Act,
    25
Communications Decency Act,
    26
communications systems
  employee misuse, 104
complicity rule, 196
compliance programs, 73-83
  attestation, 90
  benefits, 73-75, 79-80
  communications, 80, 103
  corporate culture, 73
  definitions of, 73, 80

ethics policies/codes of
    conduct, 80, 104
  internal controls/safeguards,
    80-81, 87-91
  mandates for, 73-74
  organizational due diligence
    requirements, 79-82
  proof of an effective program,
    82-83
  steps in creating, 80-82
computer-related crime
  embezzlement, 104
  fraud, 104
  malicious transmission, 111
  theft, 104
computer crime laws
  Computer Security Act, 26,
  Computer Matching and
    Privacy Act, 26
computer network, 196
computer system, 196
computers
  access controls, 129
  data backup, 91-92
  security, 91-92
condoned an offense, 196
confidentiality, 3, 196
confidentiality/secrecy
    agreements, 183-184
consequential damages, 196
conspiracy
  definition of, 155
  evidence, 155
  mail and wire fraud, 155
  prosecution of, 155
consumer confidence, 12
contracts, 197
control activities, 88, 197
control environment, 88, 197
controls,
  accounting information, 90
  behavioral considerations,
    94-99

compliance attestation, 90-91
computer, 90-92
definition of, 87-90
electronic commerce, 91-92
evaluations of, 97-98
financial, 89
inadequacies in, 98-99
internal, 91-92
management, responsibility
    for, 87-88
monitoring of, 90
protection/safeguards/
    security systems, 89-92
validity checks, 91
cookies, 5, 14, 60, 197
corporate culture, 73
credit transfers, 197
customer loyalty, 12
customer relationships, 52

damages, 197
data
    encryption, 139-140
    integrity, 197
Data Encryption Standard
    (DES), 139-141
Debt Collection Improvement
    Act, 26
digital certificates, 139
Digital Millenium Copyright
    Act, 119-121
digital pseudonyms, 112
digital signatures, 119-122,
    138
    security of, 119
    and trust, 119, 120
digital trust, 119, 142
disaster recovery, 190
    and business planning,
        190
    critical information and
        records, 190
    equipment backup, 190-191

essential procedures, 190-
    191
distributed database system,
    198
documentation, 198
Driver's Privacy Protection Act,
    9, 27
due care, 77, 80, 198
due diligence, 79, 198
duty of care, 77-78

Economic Espionage Act, 146,
    152
Eisenstadt v. Baird, 21
electronic commerce
    controls, 119
    security vulnerabilities,
        91-92
Electronic Communications
    Privacy Act, 27
electronic contracts, 119
Electronic Data Interchange
    (EDI), 137
    contracts, 137
    security, 137-139
    trading partner agreements,
        137-138
Electronic Funds Transfer Act
    (EFTA), 198
electronic record, 119, 198
electronic signatures, 119-122,
    198
embezzlement, 104
Employee Polygraph Protection
    Act, 32
Employee Retirement Income
    Security Act, 38
employees
    background inquiries, 92-94
    communications to, 80, 98,
        103-104
    infidelity, 93, 96
    screening policies, 92-94

encryption, 137-142
Equal Employment
Opportunity Act, 34
Equal Employment
Opportunity
Commission, 34
espionage, 151
ethics, 104
codes of, 104
obligations of computer
owners, 104
obligations of computer
users, 104
policies, 104
unethical behavior, 104
European Union Privacy
Protection Commission,
67
European Union Privacy
Directive, 67-69
compliance, 67-68
personal consumer
information protection,
67-68
safe harbor program, 68-69
evidence, 147, 198
extortion, 198

Fair Credit Reporting Act, 34,
52
false acceptance, 131, 198
false rejection, 131, 198
Family Education Rights and
Privacy Act, 35
Federal Contract Compliance
Regulations, 35
Federal Reserve Board, 49-51
Federal Sentencing Guidelines
for Organizations, 73-74,
76-77
Federal Trade Commission, 49,
59
authority, 49

jurisdiction, 49
privacy regulating
responsibility, 49-51
report on privacy, 7
Federal Trade Commission Act,
59
fiduciary, 161
financial institution, 49-50
financial services, 49-50
Financial Services
Modernization Act, 49-55
compliance checklist, 54-55
legal penalties, 54
privacy provisions, 51-55
fines and culpability points,
199
flagrant organizational
indifference, 199
fog index, 106
Food, Drug and Cosmetic Act,
78
foreseeability, 199

General Agreement on Tariffs
and Trade (GATT), 156
intellectual property, 156
privacy, 156
Gottschalk v. Benson, 148
Griswold v. Connecticut, 21

harassment, 111
Harvard Law Review, 21
Health Insurance Portability
and Accountability Act
(HIPPA), 41-46
health information privacy
standards, 41-46
penalties for noncompliance,
46
security of information, 41
hotlines/reporting systems in
compliance programs,
107, 180

identification, 199
identity theft, 36
Identity Theft and Assumption
    Deterrence Act, 36
indictments, 74
    U.S. Department of Justice
        guidelines, 74
information privacy products,
    12
infomediary, 10-11
insurance
    business interruption, 169
    computer crimes, 104, 169
    duty to defend, 173
    employee dishonesty, 104,
        169, 171
    employment practices, 171
    fidelity bonding, 171
    intellectual property
        infringement, 170
    Internet-specific risk policies,
        170
    insured acts, scope of, 170
    notice provision, 172
    privacy regulations, 169
    proof of loss, 172
    recovery for losses, 173
    rule of certainty, 173
    intangible assets, 170
integrity of information, 199
internal controls
    description/definition, 88
    management responsibility,
        87
Internet, 5
investigations, 81-82
    internal policy, 81, 107-108

Keeton and Prosser on Torts, 77

liability
    "black letter" law for, 76
    derivative, 78, 200

executives/directors/
    officers/corporations,
    76-77, 200
exposure inventory, 77, 177-
    183
for inadequate security, 14
for inadequate privacy
    protection, 14
negligence, 77
standards of, 78-79
strict, 78, 200
vicarious, 78, 200
loyalty economics, 10, 12-14

marketing data
    databases, 10
    gathering vs. privacy, 14-15
    research, 3-4, 14
    targeting strategies, 14
Millennium Digital Commerce
    Act, 119
monitoring, 88, 201
motivation, 201
mouse type, 11, 201

National Labor Relations Act,
    36
National Stolen Property Act,
    154-155
North American Free Trade
    Agreement (NAFTA), 156
negligence, 77, 201
nonaffiliated third party, 51-52
noncompete agreements, 164-
    165
nonpublic personal
    information, 52
nonrepudiation, 129, 201
notice, 201

Occupational Safety and Health
    Act (OSHA), 36
Omnibus Crime Control Act, 37

online alliances, 13
Open Profiling Standard, 8, 115
opt in, 4
opt out, 4, 6
ostrich instruction, 206

parity, 201
passwords, 92, 201
patents, 149
permission marketing, 3-4
policies, 103-109
   audits, 103, 109
   communications systems,
      106-107, 111-114
   compliance audits, 109
   definitions, 103
   design and development,
      103-106
   employee communications
      and education, 103-104
   enforcement and sanctions,
      108, 110-111
   ethics and codes of conduct,
      104-105
   evaluations of, 106
   investigative responses, 107-
      108
   prohibited conduct, 107
   promulgation, 106
   reporting systems, 107
   reviews of, 107
   third-party verification, 5
   violations of, 108
   websites, 114-115
polls, consumer, 4-6
portable data carriers, 128
privacy, definition and
   elements of, 3
Privacy Act, 23-24, 36
privacy legislation, 6-7, 9, 46-
   51
privacy policy, 4, 11-12, 14-17,
   109-111

privacy polls, 5
privacy-related law 6, 21-38
   common law concepts, 6, 22
privacy seals, 7-9, 114-115
"private facts," 6, 22
Private Securities Litigation
      Reform Act, 76
promulgate, 201
proprietary information, 145
   protection of, 156-157
protected health information
      (PHI), 42
prove, 202
prudent, 202
public key encryption
      infrastructure, 141-142

questioned document, 202

reasonable, 202
reckless, 202
record, 119
recordkeeping, privacy
      compliance, 16
records management, 190-194
records, trustworthy, 191
recoverability, 202
Reichheld, Frederich, 13
reliability, 202
reputational capital, 3
Reno v. Condon, 9, 27
responsible corporate officer
      doctrine, 78, 202
Right to Financial Privacy Act,
      37
risk
   analysis, 202
   assessment, 88, 203
   awareness and liability,
      105
   control, 203
   exposure, 203
   management, 203

Roe v. Wade, 6, 21
rogue employee, 203

scienter, 203
secrecy/confidentiality
     agreements, 161-164
  elements of, 162-164
  enforcement of, 165-166
Securities and Exchange
     Commission, 76
security, physical, 3, 9, 13
  technology and systems, 4
servers, 203
shrinkwrap licence, 13
signature, wet, 121
simulation and modeling, 204
smart cards, 126, 128-129
software
  copyright vs. trade secret
     protection, 148-149
  patent vs. trade secret
     protection, 149
source document, 204
spoliation, 204
*State St. Bank and Trust v.
     Signature Financial*,
     149
substantial authority
     personnel, 204

tampering, 204
Telephone Consumer
     Protection Act of 1991,
     37
Telex Corp. v. IBM Corp., 152
theft, 151
timeliness, 204
Title VII of the Civil Rights Act,
     37
tort, 77, 204
trade secrets, 145, 161
  abandonment of secrecy, 148
  concept of novelty in, 146

confidentiality in, 145-146,
     156
cost-benefit analysis, 147
definition of, 145-146, 149-
     150, 153-154
documenting loss and
     damages, 152
establishing
     misappropriation claims,
     150-151, 153
federal statutes on, 146
improper means, 151
injunctions, 151-152
law, 147-149, 152
loss of confidentiality, 148
misappropriation, 150-153
novelty, 146
protection of, 147, 156-157
recovery for damages, 152
remedies for
     misappropriation of,
     151-153
secrecy agreements, 157
tort law protection, 145,
     147-155
valuations, 147
Trade Secrets Act, 149
trading partner agreements,
     137
training/education, 80
  employees, 80
  contractors, agents, 80
transaction log, 204
trojan horse, 204
trust, 3
trust building, 9-10
trust infrastructure, 13
TRUSTe, 9
trusted third parties, 8-9
trusted transactions, 4, 10
trusting customer
     relationships, 9-10
trustmarks, 9